This book belongs to

_____

*a woman who loves
God's Word.*

Moments
of
Grace
for a
Woman's
Heart

ELIZABETH GEORGE

HARVEST HOUSE PUBLISHERS
EUGENE, OREGON

Unless otherwise indicated, all Scripture quotations are taken from the New King James Version. Copyright © 1982 by Thomas Nelson, Inc. Used by permission. All rights reserved.

Verses marked NIV are taken from the HOLY BIBLE, NEW INTERNATIONAL VERSION®. NIV®. Copyright © 1973, 1978, 1984 by the International Bible Society. Used by permission of Zondervan. All rights reserved.

Verses marked NASB are taken from the New American Standard Bible®, © 1960, 1962, 1963, 1968, 1971, 1972, 1973, 1975, 1977, 1995 by The Lockman Foundation. Used by permission. (www.Lockman.org)

Verses marked KJV are taken from the King James Version of the Bible.

Italics in Scripture quotes indicate author's emphasis.

Cover photo © Dugan Design Group, Bloomington, Minnesota

Cover by Dugan Design Group, Bloomington, Minnesota

Includes selected excerpts from A Women After God's Own Heart® Bible study series.
MOMENTS OF GRACE FOR A WOMAN'S HEART
Copyright © 2009 by Elizabeth George
Published 2013 by Harvest House Publishers
Eugene, Oregon 97402
www.harvesthousepublishers.com

ISBN 978-0-7369-5129-6 (pbk.)
ISBN 978-0-7369-5131-9 (eBook)

Printed in the United States of America

13 14 15 16 17 18 19 20 / VP-CD / 10 9 8 7 6 5 4 3 2 1

Dear Reader,

Some words really stay with you. They are so memorable and make such an impression that you never forget them. That's what happened to me when I was a brand-new Christian. Wanting to better understand my new Bible, I enrolled in a course on how to study the Bible. One evening the faithful, inspiring teacher made this statement: "A good illustration is a window into the Word of God." He went on to say that a well-crafted illustration explains the Bible text and points the way to personal application.

As a result of my time in that class, I became an avid Bible reader, Bible student, and eventually a Bible teacher. One of my goals as a teacher and creator of study materials is to write stories and create illustrations that open up the messages of the Bible so they go straight into the hearts of readers. Hopefully these writings spark "aha!" moments—moments of grace when God opens up a reader's eyes and heart to understand and embrace vital truths from His Word.

In *Moments of Grace for a Woman's Heart,* I've included many real-life stories and illustrations that are dear to my heart. They are all taken from the New Testament studies found in my Woman After God's Own Heart® Bible Study series. Just as a window brings light into a room, these stories are meant to bring light to the Scriptures in a way that highlights its truths so you can grasp their meanings and apply them to your heart.

I'm so excited you want to learn more about God's Word! I pray that these teachings and the scriptures they illustrate will stay with you, impacting your life for Christ. Hopefully they'll be a delight to your heart, bring new life to your time in God's Word, and transform your walk with Him.

In His everlasting love,

Elizabeth George

*Your word is a lamp to my feet
and a light to my path.*
PSALM 119:105

Success Made Simple

> This Book of the Law shall not depart from your mouth,
> but you shall meditate in it day and night, that you may
> observe to do according to all that is written in it.
> For then you will make your way prosperous, and then
> you will have good success.
>
> JOSHUA 1:8

Today I stood in my driveway waving to my daughter Courtney and her four children as they got ready to drive to the Navy base at Pearl Harbor. Courtney was meeting her husband to finalize their move to Hawaii. It was a beautiful day, and we'd all just witnessed a double rainbow! That incredible sight and the fact that my daughter is happily following her Navy husband as he pursues his career makes me happy too. Why?

Because Courtney, in her sometimes difficult roles of being a wife to a submariner and the mother of four small children, is following God with all her heart. That's the key to success for her. She understands and accepts the responsibilities God has given her and is being obedient and doing her best to fulfill them.

God is also asking you to follow Him wherever you are in life and in whatever you're facing day by day. How can you be successful in following Him through the many opportunities He gives you to serve and help others? Start by reading and meditating on Joshua 1:8. God is showing you the way to success—His kind of success! Joshua was in need of strength, encouragement, and wisdom for handling his assignments, his work, and his challenges. God's advice? Know the Scriptures and follow its wisdom.

If we will choose to follow God's advice, like Joshua did, God assures us of good success. As we focus fully on His Word and His promises, relying on God in everything we do, we'll experience courage, confidence, and victory.

From God's Word to Your Heart

Where does God have you today? What roles and responsibilities have been given you by your Lord? And how about your dreams and your heart's desires? Many of these indicate God's directions for your life. I encourage you to take some time to discover what the Bible says about your roles…and then pray about them. Why not jot down some dreams you have too? Write them down in your Bible, your prayer book, a personal journal, or a special notebook dedicated to dreaming and planning and doing as you become a woman after God's own heart.

God's road to success is quite simple: As you faithfully follow Him with all your heart and are obedient to fulfill His will for you, you will be blessed. You will enjoy success. Yes, you're human, and you will have moments when you fail, slide back, fall down, or stay in one place for a while. But as you rely on God and do what He asks of you through His Word and prayer, He will give you the desire and confidence—and power—to move on and enjoy life in Him.

Lord, as I look into Your Word, my heart is moved. Open my eyes to Your will. Strengthen me to step out on the path to greater faithfulness so I can better carry out Your will. Bless me in the ways You choose. Amen.

Reflecting God's Light

For you were once darkness, but now you are
light in the Lord. Walk as children of light.

EPHESIANS 5:8

Jim and I celebrated a recent anniversary on the Big Island of Hawaii, which included a trip to the famous active Kilauea Volcano. We were told to arrive at the lava flow just before dark so that we could see the most active area of red-hot lava at night. We were also warned to bring flashlights so we wouldn't fall while hiking in the dark.

As the sun began to slip into the Pacific, we started our trek over mounds of hardened lava. Right away we met a couple struggling to make the same walk without flashlights. Since we had two, we decided to give them one of ours. I can't imagine what might have happened to them if we hadn't come along with that extra flashlight.

You and I have the same need for light in the spiritual realm. Before we belonged to Christ, we were like that couple trying to walk on the path, stumbling and falling. But now we have the light of Christ! And God expects us to "let it shine," to pass on the light and be a positive influence to those still in darkness. Forget the flashlight! We have the Word of God. Ephesians 5:9 illuminates the traits we can look forward to as we walk in the light of God: goodness, righteousness, and truth.

Your desires and choices as one who walks in the light are governed by your prior determination to please God and not yourself. Each action you take needs to be prefaced by asking, "Will this be pleasing to my Lord?" If what you're considering will please God, then it's acceptable.

Christ is no longer physically present on earth, but you reflect His light to those in darkness as you bear the fruit of goodness, righteousness, truthfulness, as you seek to know God's will, as you shun the unfruitful deeds of darkness, and as you expose evil by the sheer nature of God's light in your righteous life. You are unbelievably blessed as a child of God! And as such, God says,

> You are the light of the world. A city that is set on a hill cannot be hidden. Nor do they light a lamp and put it under a basket, but on a lampstand, and it gives light to all who are in the house. Let your light so shine before men, that they may see your good works and glorify your Father in heaven (Matthew 5:14-16).

Imagine! Just as Jim and I were able to physically assist a couple walking in the dark by giving them a flashlight, you are able to do the same spiritually as you reflect the light that is yours as a child of the Supreme Light.

> *Lord, I walk in Your light with gratitude and awe. I desire to share Your light with the world by making decisions that are righteous and holy. Use me, Lord, so that I can glorify You. Amen.*

Putting On a Heart of Patience

Be patient, brethren, until the coming of the Lord.
See how the farmer waits for the precious fruit of the earth,
waiting patiently for it until it receives the early and latter
rain. You also be patient. Establish your hearts, for the
coming of the Lord is at hand.

JAMES 5:7-8

I know there are a lot of jokes made about patience ("Patience is the ability to count to ten before blasting off!" "I need patience—and I need it *now!*"), but when you're the one who's forced to wait while you suffer—or suffer while you wait—it's no laughing matter. But, my friend, as the verse above says, we need to wait patiently on the Lord.

To illustrate his point, James presents a farmer. Even if some of us don't get closer to a farm than the produce stand at a local market, we can take a look at the many ways a farmer has to employ patience. He plants his crops...and then waits for the providence of God to provide the necessary rain. Finally the early rains of the fall and the late rains of spring come.

When we're suffering, we too are to wait patiently until the coming of the Lord. How are you at waiting? Is there something God is asking you to be patient about right now?

The hope we derive from the promise of Jesus' coming helps us to wait patiently. When He arrives, He will set everything in order. He will make things right. He will correct all abuses. He will bring deliverance from our suffering. Let the certainty of the Lord's return encourage your heart as you endure hard times, moments that seem endless, and the unknowns of tomorrow.

Where is your gaze fixed? Downward...on the suffering you must endure? Or upward...in the direction from which Jesus will come? Or do you seldom think about it? Your patience will be helped when you look forward to the promise of His return. You and I live with "what is," but we have the promise of "what is to be." And in-between is the waiting time. So you can fret, worry, and pace...or you can put on a heart of patience (Colossians 3:12 NASB). Which will it be? I pray you'll choose to do what God says! "Be still [be patient], and know that I am God [the Lord who is coming again and the Judge who is indeed standing at the door]" (Psalm 46:10).

> *Lord, I'm making the decision to be still and to trust in Your promises. Today is hard, but I will wait for the rain of Your love to fall upon me. I will wait with hope for Your grace to show me the way You want me to go. Amen.*

Managing Life's Pressures

In Him we have redemption through His blood,
the forgiveness of sins, according to the riches of His grace.

Ephesians 1:7

Perhaps because our family lived in Southern California for 30-plus years, I dearly love the ocean. Surprisingly, every time I read God's Word, I think of the Pacific Ocean. I recall the many times I reveled in the sights and sounds of its surf, with the incessant splashing, crashing, sloshing-on-the-shore waves following one after another...and another...and another...and another.

Reading Ephesians 1:7 is like that repeating and splashing ocean. This verse is powerful, thrilling, and breathtaking—so spectacular it's hard to imagine another verse as exhilarating. And yet God delights in continuing to bestow His grace and His favor on us through His Son. The blessings just keep rolling in!

Another gift rolls in when we read verse 10. It's the fact of God's "dispensation" or management. He's made known "the mystery of his will...to be put into effect when the times will have reached their fulfillment" (NIV). You've probably experienced managing a household, making a master plan, and creating a time line for achieving or finishing a project. Well, my friend, God is the Master Manager, and He is organizing everything according to His timing, culminating when everything in heaven and on earth is united under Christ's leadership and authority.

Aren't you thankful for God's hand on your life? Your life is *not* hapless and purposeless. God has a plan for every step of your way. And He offers you truth and a solution for everything life throws at you...beginning with today's challenges.

From God's Word to Your Heart

Whenever your life seems to be out of control or you feel like the world and its pressures are crashing in on you, realize God is sovereign. He is in charge, and He is a faithful, flawless administrator. He is working out His good and acceptable and perfect will. His purpose in saving you and showering a continuing multitude of blessings upon you has been established.

As God's own dear child, your day and your future are secure in Him due to His kindness and mercy. God's blessings are yours! Your heart's response to God's plan of redemption for you will always be one of reveling in the truth and giving unending praise and thanksgiving to Him for all He has and will give you "according to the riches of His grace."

> *Lord, as I look into Your Word, I want to thank You for Your concern and care for the details of my life. Today has its difficulties and stress. May I be faithful to trust in Your perfect and personal management of the world around me...and me! Amen.*

Pursuing Godliness

I write so that you may know how you ought to conduct
yourself in the house of God, which is the church of the
living God, the pillar and ground of the truth. And without
controversy great is the mystery of godliness: God was
manifested in the flesh, justified in the Spirit, seen by angels,
preached among the Gentiles, believed on in the world,
received up in glory.

1 TIMOTHY 3:15-16

Have you strained to read between the lines of a letter or email
you've received? Well, the apostle Paul wanted to be sure his message to Timothy was clear, so he plainly stated its purposes. And
we get the benefit of this very direct letter about our conduct in
the church and about Christians pursuing Christlike godliness.

When Paul speaks of "the church of the living God," he is not
speaking of a building. He's describing the *people* who make up
the church. You, as a member of the church of the living God,
are part of the pillar and ground of the truth.

Paul expresses in six exquisite lines from an early church hymn
the core of the gospel and who Jesus Christ is. Let's consider each
line, remembering that every phrase is a mystery beyond our ability
to totally comprehend, yet the truths are ours to choose to believe.

God was manifested in the flesh. This is a clear reference to

Christ, who revealed the invisible God to mankind by coming to earth in human form.

He was justified in the Spirit. Here is a declaration of Christ's righteousness based on His sinless life. Jesus Christ was justified by the Holy Spirit.

He was seen by angels. The angels witnessed the entire plan of God in sending His Son Jesus to earth to redeem us and restore our relationship to Him.

He was preached among the Gentiles. This points to the worldwide proclamation of the gospel. "Go therefore and make disciples of all the nations" (Matthew 28:19).

People believed in Him. Christ is not only preached among the nations, but He is also the Redeemer and Lord and Savior to millions across the world.

He was received in glory. The apostles witnessed Jesus' ascension to heaven: "When He had spoken these things, while they watched, He was taken up, and a cloud received Him out of their sight" (Acts 1:9).

We can always be growing in our understanding of "the mystery of godliness," who is Jesus Christ.

From God's Word to Your Heart

Pursuing godliness is all about Jesus Christ. He is the mystery of godliness, the mystery once hidden but now revealed. As a believer in Christ and as a woman after God's own heart, you have the ability—and the precious privilege!—to live for Him and strive to be like Him.

Yes, you *can* live a godly life in and through Jesus Christ. Put plainly and simply, this is *piety,* a deep-seated loyalty and devotion to Christ that affects your conduct and commitment to spiritual duties and practices. What a wonderful reality! What a wonderful possession to share with others. May you and I never let the passing of time crowd out this amazing message of the awesome mystery of Christ—the hope of glory!—in us. As a woman pursuing godliness, please don't lose sight of the truth and power of the gospel of Jesus Christ.

> *Lord, I'm so thankful to grow in faith as the mystery of godliness is revealed in Jesus Christ. What a tremendous gift to be part of the living, growing, believing church that serves You. Thank You. Amen.*

Low Self-image

Blessed be the God and Father of our Lord Jesus Christ,
who has blessed us with every spiritual blessing in the
heavenly places in Christ.

EPHESIANS 1:3

I'm sure you've talked with people who suffer from a low self-image or have a "poor me" attitude. Over time I've discovered that when I'm tempted to give in to such thinking, God gives me a sure remedy. Through His Word, God's message to our hearts is to constantly remember what He's done for us through and in His Son, Jesus Christ. Let's highlight some of the riches our heavenly Father bestows on us:

- ❧ "[God] has blessed us with every spiritual blessing in the heavenly places in Christ" (Ephesians 1:3).
- ❧ "[Jesus] chose us in Him before the foundation of the world, that we should be holy and without blame before Him in love" (Ephesians 1:4).
- ❧ "God predestined you...to adoption as sons...by Jesus Christ to Himself...according to the good pleasure of His will" (Ephesians 1:5).

Aren't we fortunate! Here are some more wonderful things to contemplate.

The scope of God's blessings—You've been crowned with every spiritual blessing in Christ!

The sphere of God's blessings—Your blessings are spiritual, not material. Material blessings fade and deteriorate, but your riches in Christ are everlasting.

The source of God's blessings—You have vast spiritual wealth in Christ. As a Christian, you have all the benefits that come from having God for your heavenly Father. And you have everything you need to grow spiritually because of your relationship with Christ.

From God's Word to Your Heart

Consider the many riches God has lavished upon you. You were lost and without hope, but God in His great mercy forgave your sins through His Son's death on your behalf. Then, wonder of wonders, you were taken into God's own family and given the status of a daughter or son.

Why not pause and reflect on why God's blessings are a cure for any Christian (including you) who entertains a low self-image or "poor me" attitude. Praise God for His plan for you. Devote yourself to fulfilling His purposes. Show the world your true worth and identity as His child, "to the praise of the glory of His grace" (Ephesians 1:6).

> *Lord, as I look into Your Word, I thank You from the depths of my heart for the many spiritual blessings You've given me through Your Son Jesus. Help me recall them when I put myself down, when I think I'm inferior, and when I feel sorry for myself. Amen.*

Winning Through Winsomeness

Beloved, I beg you as sojourners and pilgrims,
abstain from fleshly lusts which war against the soul,
having your conduct honorable among the Gentiles,
that when they speak against you as evildoers, they may,
by your good works which they observe, glorify God
in the day of visitation.

1 PETER 2:11-12

Do you get frustrated by the world's lack of cooperation with your faith and your spiritual goals? Do you wonder, *Why can't the world make being pure and holy easier?* This has always been and will always be a dilemma for Christians. During Peter's time, Christians were being accused of defying Caesar, of causing social upheaval and unrest with their new religion, and of causing riots. But Pastor Peter shows believers—both then and now—how to bear up under persecution. The world won't make living your faith easy, but God's wisdom will make it easier to understand:

➤ *the world.* You and I have a status in this world that differs from that of unbelievers. We are sojourners, pilgrims, aliens, and strangers. Adjust your perspective of the world and your ties to it.

- *the Christian walk.* While we're dwelling in this strange land called earth, there are things we must do and can do to keep ourselves from sin. Put away your desires for money, power, and worldly success so that your walk isn't destroyed or marred by these temptations.

- *the why.* We're given two reasons to abstain from indulging fleshly cravings. First, so that our conduct as Christians honors Christ. When our inner life is under control, then our outer life will honor the Lord. And second, so that when critics examine our lives in order to prove our beliefs false, they will find us blameless and might be inspired to know God.

From God's Word to Your Heart

Honorable conduct. Now that's a wonderful lifetime goal! The Greek word for honorable is rich in meaning and implies the purest, highest, and noblest kind of goodness. It means "lovely," "winsome," "gracious," "noble," and "excellent." To live honorably means to live in a way that is so clean no charges against us can stand up. Attractive, gracious, upright behavior will always be our greatest defense...and our greatest witness.

Mistreatment and misunderstandings *will* come, but how you handle them speaks of your faith. Your conduct, lived out in a holy lifestyle, commends Christ to others around you. Do you have an unbelieving husband or children or parents or brothers or sisters? Do you work with non-Christians? Are you continually misunderstood because you don't think or live like the rest of "the gang"? Then rejoice that you are wearing God's soft garment of a gentle and quiet spirit! Draw it around yourself, and conduct yourself in a winsome way—a God-glorifying way.

> *God, I've never viewed the world's opposition to my beliefs as an opportunity. I've always viewed it as an obstacle. Please give me patience and a spirit of perseverance so I can overcome mistreatments and misunderstandings in ways that lead other people to a greater desire to know and understand You. Amen.*

Coping with Life's Circumstances

I know how to be abased, and I know how to abound.
Everywhere and in all things I have learned
both to be full and to be hungry, both to abound and
to suffer need. I can do all things through Christ who
strengthens me. Nevertheless you have done well that
you shared in my distress.

PHILIPPIANS 4:12-14

Who do you depend on to get through life? Are you self-sufficient like the Stoics of Paul's day? They were a group that based their ethics and morals on pride, independence, and fate. But Paul, a humble servant and "prisoner" of the Lord, considered himself to be "God-sufficient." His confidence was securely rooted in the Lord and His sovereign providence over his life. As a man who walked with Jesus, Paul could cope with anything life threw at him.

Lasting encouragement is found in the secret to contentment—knowing Jesus! So why not...

> *learn* as Paul did to endure, complete, cope with, and manage all things through Christ who will give you strength. Christ is in you, and He extends His grace and strength to you.

> *look* to the Lord for His strength. You can trust God

to bring you to and through the good plan He has for your life (Jeremiah 29:11).

- ☞ *live* out your confidence in God and rejoice in your contentment in every situation.

- ☞ *love* others by giving and sharing what you have.

No matter what you're facing, embrace life in trust and contentment based on your faith in Jesus.

From God's Word to Your Heart

What situation do you face today? Has someone you love fallen sick? Are you concerned about your child's behavior? Do you hold on to a hurt from the past? Just as Christ's strength is sufficient for all you endure, it is sufficient to get you through each day.

Dear one, not one day goes by that I don't remind myself of the awesomeness of God and His provisions for me and the ones I love. As His child you can look to Him, His Word, His promises, and His strength, and He will graciously—every time and without fail!—provide what you need for taking one more step along your God-ordained path. In fact, tell yourself, "I can do *all* things [including this] through Christ who strengthens me" (Philippians 4:13). How blessed you are to be able to turn to and trust God in every circumstance for every need.

Lift up Paul's words in Philippians 4:13 as your personal promise. There is no need to just cope when you have the Lord!

> *God, I give today's trouble to You. With renewed hope,*
> *I exchange my independence for God dependence. I will*
> *stop striving to be self-sufficient so that I can embrace the*
> *hope and peace of being God-sufficient. Amen.*

Are You Ready?

Now as He drew near, He saw [Jerusalem] and wept over it, saying, "If you had known, even you, especially in this your day, the things that make for your peace! But now they are hidden from your eyes."

LUKE 19:41-42

In Oklahoma, where I grew up, Palm Sunday was significant for two reasons. First of all, I knew when this special Sunday rolled around that winter was over...and spring was here to stay. Second, and more importantly, this was the day we remembered Jesus' entry into Jerusalem. In my little church each person received small palm branches or fronds when they entered the building. There were special songs and a sermon describing Jesus' journey to Jerusalem and, ultimately, to the cross.

As you and I contemplate the first Palm Sunday, we can discover from Jesus what to focus on and take in so our faith in Him will grow. Reread today's verse. Notice what's in Jesus' heart as He draws near Jerusalem:

> ☞ His focus is on those who did not receive Him. Jesus is heartbroken over those souls who do not recognize Him as the Messiah. He weeps for those who turn from Him.

☞ His focus is *not* on the fate that awaits Him. His weeping is not for His personal anguish and sacrifice. Instead, it's for those who are not yet part of His kingdom.

Each day is precious when we consider what we can do to serve God and His kingdom. Why not make a list of the many ways you can share the good news with others? Where is your focus?

From God's Word to Your Heart

Whenever we read the dramatic end of the Gospel of Luke, we're hushed as we realize that the final week of Jesus' life on earth has arrived. Our Lord has steadfastly prepared for this specific time. Even at the tender age of 12, He knew His purpose: "Did you not know that I must be about My Father's business?" (Luke 2:49). Three short years after He began His ministry at the age of 30, Jesus had inflamed a nation with His passion. He faithfully taught His disciples. He tirelessly addressed the multitudes. He miraculously healed individuals. And He consistently angered the Jewish religious leaders.

Yet as He entered Jerusalem, Jesus wept. He knew the Jewish people were not looking for a spiritual Savior. They were looking for a conquering hero who would return their nation to glory. How about you? Are you searching for meaning in the right places? Are you frustrated, defeated, and about out of hope? Are you looking for Someone to make your life meaningful today and for eternity? Recognize and embrace Christ as your Messiah! Make it a priority to prepare yourself for the King and His kingdom. Be ready!

Lord, You have such a heart for Your children. Thank You for loving me and caring about my life. I want to serve You and honor You in everything I do. Also, as I go out and about today, help me recognize and love those who don't know You. Give me the wisdom and boldness to share with them what will give them peace now and forever—You! Amen.

Living in the Shadow of Eternity

The end of all things is at hand;
therefore be serious and watchful in your prayers.
And above all things have fervent love for one another,
for "love will cover a multitude of sins."

1 PETER 4:7-8

Have you stood in your church sort of dreamily singing along to the hymn "Jesus Is Coming Again"? All creation yearns and waits for that wonderful day when Jesus returns to right all wrongs and heal the ravages of sin. We're on our way to eternity, but until then, you and I face all the challenges of being in the world today. So how do we best live in the shadow of eternity? How should the nearness of Jesus Christ's return affect our daily lives?

We are called by God to be serious so we won't be swept away by emotions or passions. We are also to be in watchful pursuit of holiness, being like sojourners passing through this life on our way to our ultimate goal—heaven. How do we do this? Prayer is our stabilizer, our constant reminder, our way to maintain these two attitudes. We can pray today for a godly and eternal perspective that will influence our daily lives for holy living.

Have you wondered what God's priorities are? Well, right in

1 Peter 4:8, God reminds us of His priority #1 for our relationships with others in the church: "Above all things, have fervent love for one another." We can love beyond human limits by loving with the heart of Jesus.

From God's Word to Your Heart

Has today's Scripture verses moved you in a fresh and new way? It's so simple—and so simply stated. It leaves no doubt about who you are and what you're to focus on and do. I don't know about you, but this is exactly the kind of clear-cut instruction that my heart yearns for. You can take these words to heart and put them to work. How, you ask?

Regarding self—Be more alert to eternal perspective. Battle the natural tendency to get wrapped up in this world. Don't set your affection on the things of this earth, such as possessions, social status, and investment portfolios. Instead, focus your attention and desires on things above: "Whatever things are true, whatever things are noble, whatever things are just, whatever things are pure, whatever things are lovely, whatever things are of good report, if there is any virtue and if there is anything praiseworthy—meditate on these things" (Philippians 4:8).

Regarding others—With the heart of Christ, be aware of your responsibilities to God's people. Love as a good steward of the amazing grace God has given to you. God wants your life and love to be centered on Him and His people, not on things of this world. His call is to love, to lodge, and to look out for your brothers and sisters in Christ.

I know you want your life spent here on earth to mean something and to bring glory to God. Thank the Lord for showing you *how* in His Word!

Father, I look to You for Your grace and Your strength. As I live in the shadow of eternity, help me embrace all that today offers that has its roots in You. I want to learn more about You, serve and love others more, and offer my praise to You every day. Amen.

Handling Riches

Command those who are rich in this present age not to be haughty, nor to trust in uncertain riches but in the living God, who gives us richly all things to enjoy. Let them do good, that they be rich in good works, ready to give, willing to share, storing up for themselves a good foundation for the time to come, that they may lay hold on eternal life.

1 TIMOTHY 6:17-19

Today you and I get to sit in the front row at the apostle Paul's money management seminar and learn firsthand how to handle what God has blessed us with...*God's* way. Now, Paul doesn't condemn believers for their riches, but he is warning them (and us) to handle what they have wisely so they can develop spiritual wealth and enjoy eternal life. What principles does Paul promote?

Principle 1: Avoid the temptations of the wealthy. Do not become arrogant and place your trust in earthly riches instead of in the living God.

Principle 2: Engage in the duties for those of means. Be rich in good works, be prepared to give, and be willing to share.

Principle 3: Resist laying up treasures for yourself. Share earthly treasures, and *then* you will lay hold of eternal life. Salvation doesn't come by giving your wealth away. You must put your faith and trust in Jesus Christ. But the fruit of your salvation will be seen in your attitude toward others.

Principle 4: Lay hold of good works. Giving doesn't require money. Many of the men and women of the Bible who gave were poor. Even if you have little to give, follow in the footsteps of their good works.

There's a lot to learn about how you relate to money by going to one specific source—your checkbook. Your attitude and priorities are there in black and white. Are you a spender? A giver? A hoarder? A saver?

When you look at your check register, what tale is told regarding your heart and your values and your way of handling finances? Take note of the checks you've written during the past month. Did your treasure go to some shops at the mall...or to help people? Was your treasure spent for curtains...or for the church? Many of you may be surprised to find that your spending doesn't reflect the heart of love and sharing you want to have.

Was that a revealing exercise for you? The first time I did it, it was for me. God may not be asking you to sell or give away all your possessions and wealth. But He is definitely asking you to prayerfully consider how you handle the riches He's given you. You are *so* blessed, and now you can bless others.

> *God, help me be a cheerful giver. I see the needs around me and hear of more every day. I want to honor You with my attitudes and actions regarding how I spend and share the financial and material blessings You've given me. Remind me to release my hold on earthly treasures. I know my heart will reap the rewards of joyously giving in Your name. Amen.*

Overcoming Anxiety

Rejoice in the Lord always. Again I will say, rejoice!

PHILIPPIANS 4:4

Most women create "to do" lists that show what they need to do that day, that week, that month. These catalogs of tasks, phone calls, reminders, and plans keep us on track so we get more done and better manage the events of day-to-day life. We might have other forms of organization, but few methods keep us so focused.

If you could borrow anyone's "to do" list, I suggest you take a look at the apostle Paul's. In the book of Philippians one of his recurring themes is peace. So Paul's "to do" list shows us how to enjoy the peace that is available to us as believers in Christ. You see, Paul so greatly desired peace among members of the body of Christ that he exhorts each person to possess the personal peace God offers. Only then can there be harmony in the church. In 4:5-6 he writes:

- "Let your gentleness be known to all men." Be forgiving and fair and gracious.
- "Be anxious for nothing." Trust in the Lord, and hope and peace will follow.
- "Let your requests be made known to God." Exercise your faith and give your needs to God.

When we think of all we want in life, I know joy ranks high. So does peace. And here, in the God-breathed, inspired Word that comes straight from the mind and heart of God, we have the source of both! But to enjoy these two desired qualities of life, we must follow the list with devotion. What does this look like? What are we to do?

Rejoice. This is not optional, my friend. This is a command. It's an exhortation to cheerfulness. "Rejoice in the Lord always. Again I will say, rejoice!" (verse 4). We are to rejoice *in the Lord,* no matter what is happening to us.

Pray. This too is not optional…it's a command. Rather than suffering from anxiety, we are to present our needs to the Lord and trust Him to provide for us. In any and all circumstances, we are to lay our requests before God and trust Him to take care of us.

And the results? The sweet, sweet results? First, not only will God respond to our prayers, but we'll experience "the peace of God"—the peace that is characteristic of God Himself. Even when our difficult circumstances don't change, God's peace will prevail. Second, God's peace will stand guard over us, like a soldier or a sentinel, protecting us against the anxieties and worries that want to attack our hearts and minds. Through prayer we will truly experience God's peace that surpasses all human comprehension.

> *Lord, I'm ready to create a "to do" list of joy and peace.*
> *Thank You for Paul's example. I lift up my needs to You*
> *and trust in You. You calm my fears. You guide my steps.*
> *You lead me to Your presence. I am rejoicing in You! Amen.*

Spiritual Insights

I also, after I heard of your faith in
the Lord Jesus and your love for all the saints,
do not cease to give thanks for you,
making mention of you in my prayers.

EPHESIANS 1:15

When we love people, we can't help but pray for them because we carry them in our hearts. And when friends are far away and we're unable to express our love and support personally, we can pray knowing that God hears us. Jesus prayed for His disciples. Paul prayed for the believers in Philippi, the Christians in Colossae, and for his friends in Ephesus. When it comes to your friends and friendships, there are many reasons to turn to God in prayer! What can you do?

Praise God for your friends. You've been blessed with special people in your life. Give thanks for them.

Pray for their spiritual well-being and insights. Paul prayed for believers to have their spiritual eyes opened so they would recognize their spiritual blessings.

Pray for the body of Christ, the church. Pray for your friends to make Jesus the Lord and Savior of their lives. And give thanks for Christ and His leadership.

Every prayer you lift up for your friends and for others who are placed on your heart reaches God's ears and heart. Ask Him to use His power, might, strength, and wisdom to help the people you care about.

Paul was a prisoner when he wrote with such conviction about compassionate prayer for others. You would expect an innocent prisoner to rant, rave, blame others, question God, and sink into depression. But not Paul. He praised God! His outbursts of worship and lists of blessings run through his entire letter to the believers in Philippi. The overflow of Paul's heart is evidence that he meditated on God's sovereign plan, the Holy Spirit's indwelling, Jesus' supremacy, and the shining effects of God's grace.

Pray as Paul did! No matter your circumstances or your troubles, ask God to help you and the people in your life develop "spiritual eyes" for seeing and understanding your riches and blessings in Jesus Christ. Tell Him you want to...

- know Him better
- look with great hope and anticipation to His upward calling
- understand your special relationship as His child and heir
- experience His power moment by moment in your life

What are your difficult circumstances today? You might be limited by a life situation, but God is never hampered. Praise Him!

Why not write a few words of hope and comfort to a loved one who needs encouragement? Or call someone who needs God's peace and pray with him or her. And share spiritual insights from God's Word.

Lord, thank You for hearing my prayers for my friends. For those who don't know You, help me be an example of Your love and grace. And for those friends who know You, I pray they will see Your hand in their lives. May we all give You glory. Amen.

Favoritism

Do not hold the faith of our Lord Jesus Christ,
the Lord of glory, with partiality.

JAMES 2:1

Have you been on the negative end of favoritism? Snubbed with a haughty sneer? Ignored when you arrived at an event? Abruptly bumped out of the way by another as he or she rushed to speak to someone else? Passed over by a group or a committee?

If so, you know the pain of partiality. And what's worse is that being human, we've probably dished out partiality ourselves! That is such a painful truth. It seems that no matter what our status is, there are always others who are better looking, wealthier, and more talented than we are...and there are always others who "fall beneath us" in some way. It seems like we spend our lives looking up at some and down on others.

The truth is that there is no positive side of favoritism. That is why James points us to a better, indeed, a glorious standard. That standard of impartiality and equality is set by Jesus. The New International Version of the Bible translates James 2:1 this way: "As believers in our glorious Lord Jesus Christ, don't show favoritism."

In case we question the standard laid out for us in today's verse, James presents a fictionalized (or was it?) church meeting with two kinds of visitors: a rich, "gold-fingered" man in fine, bright, gorgeous clothing, and a poor man in dirty, smelly clothes. Let's take a closer look at this powerful example of how favoritism can prevent us from living our faith.

If there should come into your assembly a man with gold rings, in fine apparel, and there should also come in a poor man in filthy clothes, and you pay attention to the one wearing the fine clothes and say to him, "You sit here in a good place," and say to the poor man, "You stand there," or, "Sit here at my footstool," have you not shown partiality among yourselves, and become judges with evil thoughts? (James 2:2-4).

The message is certainly clear, isn't it? We aren't honoring God and living His way if we treat anyone with partiality or favoritism. Such behavior is contradictory and incompatible with our salvation, which was accomplished by an impartial God who extended His love toward all of us by sending His Son to die for our sins and redeem us so we could experience a personal relationship with Him.

Father, may I never show favoritism because of perceived wealth, success, or influence. Keep me from a heart that is jaded by the world's standards or my own sense of entitlement. Guard my heart so I will be content in You. Give me a heart of love for all people so I can tell them about You. Amen.

Making the Most of Opportunity

No servant can serve two masters; for either he will
hate the one and love the other, or else he will be loyal
to the one and despise the other. You cannot serve God
and mammon [money].

LUKE 16:13

Whether we acknowledge it or not, nothing that is ours is truly ours. Our homes, our finances, our husbands, our children, our health...and ultimately our lives...belong to God. A steward is "one who is accountable to another." In our case, we answer to God for all He entrusts us with. Keep in mind these words from the apostle Paul: "It is required in stewards that one be found faithful" (1 Corinthians 4:2).

Are you faithful? Which representation of worldly wealth is your biggest obstacle to godly stewardship? Your house? Your possessions? For many of us it's money. Here is God's wisdom: "Where your treasure is, there your heart will be also" (Matthew 6:21). Stored riches on earth will break down and can be stolen. But those treasures we place in heaven will be preserved forever. Our minds need to focus on the eternal:

Instruct those who are rich in this present world not to be
conceited or to fix their hope on the uncertainty of riches,
but on God, who richly supplies us with all things to enjoy.

Instruct them to do good, to be rich in good works, to be generous and ready to share, storing up for themselves the treasure of a good foundation for the future, so that they may take hold of that which is life indeed (1 Timothy 6:17-19 NASB).

We are to place all our trust in God alone. When we do experience a season blessed with financial security, we have the opportunity to use it to help others. We can give richly, serve sacrificially, and love unconditionally...as we follow Jesus' example.

From God's Word to Your Heart

Everyone wonders about life after death. In the Gospel of Luke, we have a parable Jesus told that gives us a possible glimpse of life beyond this earth. A beggar dies and enters a life of comfort after an earthly existence of torment. We also read about the death of a rich man who lived his days on earth in splendor...and woke up to eternal torment in Hades. What made the difference? We can infer that the rich man didn't heed the Word of the Lord or seek the instruction of God. He didn't reach out to help the poor and downtrodden. Instead, he lived in luxury, concentrating on worldly wealth. Lazarus, the beggar, was humble and content to eat what fell from the rich man's table. When he died he was rewarded by being brought into heaven.

My friend, clearly the ultimate stewardship you're given is your life on earth. How can you use it to be a better servant of God and glorify Him?

God, help me make the most of the opportunities You bring my way today. I want to be rich in good works for You. Replace my longing for earthly treasures with hope and peace and a desire for heavenly blessings. Amen.

Responding Responsibly

Gird up the loins of your mind, be sober,
and rest your hope fully upon the grace that is to be
brought to you at the revelation of Jesus Christ.

1 PETER 1:13

We've been granted great blessings from the mind and heart of God. Not only do we enjoy the new birth and the living hope found in our living Savior, but we also possess the glorious inheritance that is ours and the protection of God. The way we live is a response to these blessings of faith. Peter presents a sort of "to do" list for those of us who belong to the Lord and desire to make His characteristics ours.

- "Gird up the loins of your mind" is Peter's reminder for us to always be mentally prepared for whatever comes our way. We can do this by immersing ourselves in God's Word and by asking for His wisdom and guidance.

- "Be sober" encourages us to put aside self-indulgence and practice self-control and discipline. When our lives are marked by sobriety, we can act with clarity of mind because our focus is on Christ.

- "Rest your hope fully upon the grace…of Jesus" tells us to set our minds on God's plans for us, change our lifestyles to glorify Him, and persevere during and through the trials that come. When our hope is in the Lord, we can be confident in every arena of our lives.

🖝 "Be holy" reminds us to put aside the lusts and sins that were previously part of our lives. Our noble, righteous goal now is to live a Christ-filled life.

From God's Word to Your Heart

Doesn't it stand to reason that what's on the inside should and must come out? When God comes to live in us, shouldn't our lives change? And when we contemplate the price Jesus Christ paid for our redemption, shouldn't this result in faithful obedience to Him? Scripture reveals all that is given to us and happens to us on the inside when we're born again—the new birth, the inheritance, and the fact that we are kept for heaven and heaven is kept for us. Such wonders ought to make a radical difference in us.

As a Christian you've been granted a position in Christ. You are called to God, chosen by God, saved by God, and declared holy as belonging to God. Therefore, live responsibly. Live for God! May you, as a woman of God, set your mind to work on incorporating His divine likeness in your life today.

Lord, I want to make Your characteristics my own. May my actions and words honor Your love and sacrifice. Your presence and grace have transformed me. Out of gratitude, I pray to be faithful and obedient to Your calling. Amen.

Fruits of Faithfulness

Some men's sins are clearly evident, preceding them to
judgment, but those of some men follow later. Likewise,
the good works of some are clearly evident, and those that
are otherwise cannot be hidden.

1 TIMOTHY 5:24-25

Have you earned a godly reputation? It's been said that a
good reputation takes a lifetime to develop but can be lost in a
moment. That's why it's so vital that you and I adhere to God's
instructions in His Word and clearly understand how to model
godly behavior. In Scripture we're taught the principles of a leader.
These are excellent characteristics to develop whether we're in
official positions of leadership or not.

As Christians, we are Christ's representatives. And we never
know when someone is looking at us and making judgments about
Christ based on our actions. That's reason enough to seek instruction from the apostle Paul! We want to be blameless examples of
Christ's love and honor.

Two principles stand out in today's Scripture verses that speak
clearly to every Christian pursuing godliness. Before we have any
part in evaluating leaders...or anyone else, we must take care to
examine ourselves first.

Principle 1: Sin cannot be hidden. Paul says sin will be evident...
sooner or later. As you examine your heart, is there any area of

sin you need to confess and forsake? If so, what are your plans to do so? Remember, "If we confess our sins, He is faithful and just to forgive us our sins and to cleanse us from all unrighteousness" (1 John 1:9).

Principle 2: Good works cannot be hidden. Even if they're not instantly acknowledged, they will eventually come to light (1 Timothy 5:25). And remember that we're to do good works for God's glory, not our personal gain or recognition. Queen Esther's cousin Mordecai thwarted a plot to harm the king, probably saving the king's life. For five years his act of service went unrewarded (Esther 6:1-3). How would you handle going that long without being acknowledged or thanked for a good deed?

From God's Word to Your Heart

Reading 1 Timothy 5:24-25 feels a bit like we're eavesdropping on a private father/son talk between Paul and Timothy, doesn't it? Or maybe we're reading the minutes to a very high-level meeting. Timothy is a pastor, and Paul is a teacher's teacher. And the apostle is giving straightforward direction to his young protégé.

The Bible gives you and me straightforward direction too about our conduct. Here are a few do's and don'ts to take to heart:

- *Do* examine your own life.
- *Do* pursue godliness.
- *Do* pray for purity in your leadership.
- *Do* trust God with the lives and actions of others.
- *Don't* be a part of causing trouble in the church.
- *Don't* be a part of gossiping and tearing down the hard-won reputations of others.

Make sure you put your time and commitment toward actions

and words that are good. May those be revealed in time as fruits of a faithful life.

God, there are people in my life who are watching my behavior. I'm responsible for the example of Christ they are witnessing. Help me hold to godly, principled behavior so that I serve You with integrity. Amen.

Living in Unity

I implore Euodia and I implore Syntyche to be of the
same mind in the Lord. And I urge you also, true
companion, help these women who labored with me in
the gospel, with Clement also, and the rest of my fellow
workers, whose names are in the Book of Life.

Philippians 4:2-3

Have you been at odds with another person in your church?
Have two of your Christian friends ever started an argument
while you were present...and you weren't sure what to do? You
and I can learn a lot if we pay attention to how Paul, the master
motivator, handled it. Reread Paul's note about this type of situation in today's verses. Does it sound sadly familiar? Paul desired
peace among believers, and apparently the differences between
these two women in the church were affecting the spirit of fellowship and harmony that should characterize the people of God.

Whether you're the one in the disagreement or you're the one
who is helping to lead the parties back to unity, gently approach
the other party with reconciliation in your heart and on your mind.

From God's Word to Your Heart

Euodia and Syntyche, two of Paul's friends and coworkers for
the cause of Christ, were having differences. The rift between

them was affecting those around them. So how did Paul handle the problem? There is much here for us to learn.

Paul spoke directly to the two ladies (and anyone else who may have been involved in strife), imploring them to settle their dispute and live in harmony. Wisely, Paul based his appeal on the cause of Christ. He asked that they be of the same mind "in the Lord," that they keep the peace, that they live in love. They were to put aside their differences for the grander cause of the common good of the church at Philippi and the body of Christ.

Paul praised these two women. Paul recalls how they labored shoulder-to-shoulder with him for the cause of the gospel. He also reminds them that they served with Clement and the rest of the workers for Christ.

Paul called upon others in the church to help Euodia and Syntyche. He encouraged their involvement in helping to solve the problem. These women had helped others, and now others needed to help them.

My friend, pray! Pray that you won't be the cause of any disruptions in your church and that you won't hinder the work of the church for the cause of Christ. Ask God to help you follow in Paul's wise footsteps if you have the opportunity to help solve a dispute between others. Ask Him to help you live in unity.

God, please keep me from being a division in Your body of believers. Help me follow Paul's words and actions to bring unity and harmony to those around me. I want to be a peacekeeper in Your name. Amen.

Leaving the Old Life Behind

Lay aside the old self, which is being corrupted in accordance with
the lusts of deceit, and...be renewed in the spirit of your mind,
and put on the new self, which in the likeness of God has been
created in righteousness and holiness of the truth.

EPHESIANS 4:22-24 NASB

For a sum of money, you can find a salon that will give you a
new hairdo, an updated wardrobe, and a new physical presence.
But there is only one being who can change someone from the
inside out—to truly create a new person, with godly character,
values, attitudes, perspectives, and motives. That, of course, is God.

When you became a believer, you entered into an intimate,
personal relationship with Jesus. When you embraced Him as
Savior, you put into motion a lifelong process of putting off the
sin-marred ways of mankind and donning the nature and conduct
of a new creation in Christ. Dear one, this is the most amazing,
luxurious, transforming makeover you can imagine!

As part of the process, the bad attitudes and habits you've
added to your life over the years start falling by the wayside as
you're filled with the love and power of Jesus. With God's help,
you begin to get rid of those attitudes that are far from flattering
and don't fit anymore—selfishness, anger, ignorance, impatience,
envy, and so forth. You toss these out of your closet of choices

and discover, instead, how to dress in the wonderful attributes God enables you to wear, including His knowledge and wisdom.

In light of putting off and putting on, do any behaviors, faults, shortcomings, or areas of sin pop immediately into your mind? Turn these over to Jesus immediately. A Christian who possesses new life in Christ is different, is set apart from the world. You are now the temple of the Holy Spirit. So let the Master's makeover begin!

From God's Word to Your Heart

Your Master is calling for action. You are to stop living a purposeless life. You have been miraculously raised from the dead! There is no need or reason to live as the unsaved live. Live as the daughter of the King of kings! And you don't have to do this on your own strength. Jesus will help you...if you only ask! So start every morning by talking to Him, asking Him to guide you and give you strength to live for Him. Leave the old life behind. Study His Word and incorporate His wisdom and principles into your daily life. You might not recognize yourself after this makeover!

Lord, I am a new creation in You. But I've held on to some clothing from my past...sins, failures, and worldly attitudes. Drape me in the wonderful fabric of Your nature and Your love. Help me become a new woman in You. Thank You. Amen.

Submitting to Authority

A windstorm came down on the lake, and [the boat was]
filling with water, and [they] were in jeopardy. And they
came to Him and awoke Him, saying, "Master, Master, we
are perishing!" Then He arose and rebuked the wind and
the raging of the water. And they ceased, and there was a
calm. But He said to them, "Where is your faith?"

LUKE 8:23-25

Over and over we read about submission to authority in the
Bible. Recognizing and submitting to authority is no easy assign-
ment for any of us. We want to be in control of our lives and
circumstances...at least until a crisis comes along.

Jesus shows us His divine control over all things so we know
we can trust Him with our lives and all its ups and downs. The
Son of Man has authority over nature, demons, disease, and death.
When the disciples were in the boat with Jesus, and the storms
came and the waters began to rush into the boat, they ran to Him.
They didn't trust that God was already in control of the situation.
Their lack of faith was evident in their fear. They cried out, "We
are perishing!" No wonder Jesus asks them, "Where is your faith?"

You and I are to *ask* for help and then *believe.* If we are living
in submission to God and His will, when the storms come upon
us we won't ride waves of fear but will immediately rest in the
calm of faith in Jesus.

Don't wait until the boat is sinking to recognize His authority and call for help. Submit now and marvel at the ministry of the Son of Man in your life. You'll be amazed by the peace, contentment, and love that will flood your life.

From God's Word to Your Heart

One of the most heartwarming accounts in the Gospels comes in Luke 8. Because of demons, a certain man was kept shackled and under guard. But he broke loose and was living in the wilderness, running around naked. He was in a hopeless condition. But he met Jesus, and Jesus commanded the unclean spirits to leave the man's body. As a result, he was healed! He became calm. Donning some clothes, he now sat in his right mind at the feet of Jesus.

But the story doesn't end there. Wanting to follow Jesus, he instead submitted to the Lord's authority and did as He asked: "Return to your own house, and tell what great things God has done for you." And what about the newly delivered man's passion? "He went his way and proclaimed throughout the whole city what great things Jesus had done for him" (verse 39).

Are you faithfully submitting to authority and following through on one of your purposes—telling others about God? Ask Jesus to revitalize your passion for sharing with others about what He's done in your life.

Lord, I will point others to You today as I express my joy in having my life submitted to Your might and authority. I will tell of the great things You've done for me. If there are areas in my life that I still need to submit to You, please reveal them to me. I want to dedicate all of me to You. Amen.

Speaking with Wisdom

My brethren, let not many of you become teachers,
knowing that we shall receive a stricter judgment.

JAMES 3:1

Have you considered being a teacher? Perhaps becoming a
Bible-study leader or a spiritual mentor to another woman? I
love to hear women express their hearts by serving God in these
ways. Many of us came to know Christ because another woman
joyfully took on the challenge and responsibility of reaching out
in Christ. Notice that I didn't call teaching a "simple task" or an
"easy act of discipline." That would be misleading. By looking at
God's Word, we discover that God takes the role of teacher very
seriously...and so should we.

As today's verse shows, there is a stricter judgment for those
who take on the extraordinary role of instructing others in God's
Word, matters of faith, and the foundations of Christian living.
If you are or want to be a teacher of God's truth, make sure your
motives are pure and free from selfish ambition. If you feel called
of God to reach out to others, then step out in faith, knowing He'll
guide you and be with you. Be constantly in prayer, and prepare
for your responsibilities by studying the Word. You'll experience
great blessings as you follow through and do as God asks you.

It's a good idea to pause right now as you're contemplating teaching and teachers and remember those who have faithfully and accurately taught you. Indeed, they took a great risk (in light of James 3:1) each and every time they opened their mouths.

- *Your pastor.* Thank God for his diligent study and for seeking to rightly divide God's Word and teach its truths clearly (2 Timothy 2:15).

- *Your parents.* They imparted to you skills, values, and instructions for life. And, if they're Christians, think of how they introduced you to God, to His Son, to the Holy Spirit, and to the Bible. In most situations there is *something* your parents taught you that you can thank the Lord for.

- *Schoolteachers and professors.* They, like a candle, extend light to others by consuming themselves. God uses these dedicated souls to enlighten our lives.

- *Older women.* Mentors have unselfishly taken time to share with you, to encourage you, to instruct you, and to train you in the good things of the Lord.

May you use your tongue to speak with wisdom to those who struggle in darkness. Ask God to give you "the tongue of the learned" so that you can freely give a word of encouragement and instruction to those who are weary (Isaiah 50:4).

> *Lord, thank You for those who modeled faith and godly wisdom to me during my life. If You lead me to take on the responsibility of helping to shepherd another person, I will take that calling seriously. Please grant me Your wisdom as I'm faithful to follow You in this way. Amen.*

Ministering Faithfully

Their wives must be reverent,
not slanderers, temperate,
faithful in all things.

1 TIMOTHY 3:11

I especially love this verse about the role of women in the church to women in the church. In my home church, women involved in this ministry are called deaconesses. It was my privilege to serve in this capacity for more than 20 years.

As the early church grew, new needs arose. Who would teach the new female believers? Who would counsel them regarding marriage and family problems? Who would tend to them in childbirth, illness, and preparing for death? Who would visit them in their homes? The women!

Understanding the behaviors of these early church women is a way to understand how you and I are to serve the body of Christ. What characteristics are we, as faithful servants, to have?

Reverent and dignified—Since God is first and foremost in the heart of every woman who pursues godliness, hers is a life of worship. As the daughter of the King, act with nobility of purpose, dignity, and decorum.

Not slanderers—A person who talks maliciously about others is called a *gossip*. Helping women by our works and hurting women by our words *do not* go together. Be careful what you share with others. Make sure your motives are pure, you're not violating a trust, and God will be honored by your actions.

Temperate—Temperance is more than a call to abstain from excess. It's also an emotional calling to be calm, dispassionate, grave, and sober in knowing God's Word and its truths. It's a call to self-control, to be free from addiction to anything. This doesn't mean you can't be passionate and vibrant in your faith.

Faithful in all things—A servant in the church must also be reliable and completely trustworthy as he or she carries out the business of the church.

This is our call, my sister in Christ. We're to live out our love for Christ by faithfully performing our God-given duties according to the instructions we receive.

From God's Word to Your Heart

Is faithfully serving God one of the deep-seated desires of your heart? Faithfulness is a beautiful quality. Jesus spoke often of it. The apostle Paul required it of himself and those who ministered with him. And Timothy exemplified it. Take a moment now and ask God to assist you in being "faithful in all things" in your everyday life. No matter how big (service in the church) or small (quiet deeds done at home), minister faithfully.

Faithfulness is a wonderful quality! May your devotion to God be evident in all that you say and do so that God's life in you can't be missed.

> *Lord, are my words uplifting to others? Are my actions honorable and selfless? Every morning help me devote my day to You—my Father, my King, my Lord. Amen.*

Growing in Him

Laying aside all malice, all deceit, hypocrisy, envy, and all
evil speaking, as newborn babes, desire the pure milk of the
word, that you may grow thereby, if indeed you have tasted
that the Lord is gracious.

1 PETER 2:1-3

Are you thirsty? Are you craving time in God's Word? Peter
instructs us to yearn for the Word of God as a baby needs milk.
This reflects the way our longing should feel as we thirst for knowledge of God. It's also a lovely reminder that studying God's Word
should never be a labor; it should always be a delight. Filling up
on God's promises and instructions is a satisfying, nourishing,
enlightening experience.

One way to delight in the maturing of your faith is to take an
inventory of your current life. Have you ever faced an overflowing closet and made the decision to get rid of those things that
are torn or no longer fit? Believe me, it's not easy to part with
those things you are familiar with, but the trade-off in orderliness, ease in finding items, and knowing what is there is worth
it. Take the same approach to your spiritual life. Roll up your
sleeves and discard these attitudes and behaviors that have no
place in a believer's life:

- *Guile or deceit*—deliberately tricking and/or misleading others by lying

- *Hypocrisy*—saying one thing and doing another

- *Envy*—discontent and resentment arising from someone else having something you want

- *Evil speaking*—slander, gossip, rumor-spreading, and ruining the reputation of another

Whew! It's good to have those gone. Now add those things that are uplifting and life-giving: God's Word and His truth. As a child of God, concentrate on learning and growing and maturing in Christ.

From God's Word to Your Heart

Beloved, it's never too late to grow in the Lord. It's never too late to discard behaviors that are unlike your God. And it's never too late to embrace the spiritual truths found in God's Word. Discarding the bad and desiring the good can be actions you take each and every day of your life. Even believers of 10, 20, or 30 years still crave the Word of God. In fact, the desire increases the more you grow in Christ! Oh, how I hope and pray this is true of you!

We are called to discard and to desire. I used to struggle with gossiping. But through consistent prayer, accountability, and the desire to be like Christ, I was finally able to eliminate gossip from my life. I encourage you to purge whatever is not righteous and good in your life too. You'll have times of relapse—we all do. But persevere!

Lord, I'm ready to purge gossip and other negative uses of my voice from my life with Your strength. I can't believe I've become so comfortable with these useless and hurtful things. I'm ready to discard them and to replace them with the truth of Your Word. Help me grow in You every day. Amen.

Following God's Design for Family

Children, obey your parents in the Lord, for this is
right. "Honor your father and mother," which is the first
commandment with promise: "that it may be well with you
and you may live long on the earth." And you, fathers, do
not provoke your children to wrath, but bring them up in
the training and admonition of the Lord.

Ephesians 6:1-4

If you're a mom, you know the fear that comes when your
child falls at the playground or when you haven't heard from
your teenager after curfew. In the Roman world of Paul's day,
life was even more fearful for mothers and perilous for children.
Many children were abandoned, sold into slavery, or neglected
by their families. Roman law gave the father absolute power. If
the father was a tyrant, his wife and children could be subjected
to a lifetime of cruelty. This is why Paul's remarkable image of
a Spirit-filled family offered hope and continues to serve as a
model of a godly family for us today. The encouragement and
instruction of God's Word is always relevant.

The attributes we are to instill in all of our relationships are
obedience and honor. Children will especially follow your example
as you are faithful to...

⚘ discipline	⚘ keep love as the foundation
⚘ encourage	⚘ nurture
⚘ instruct	⚘ praise

Your family will flourish when decisions are guided by the Lord—the head of your household.

Generally, because of the amount of time you spend with your children compared to your husband, you are on the front line of parenthood. Your influence is great, but don't fail to include your husband in the parenting process. Make it a goal to work as a team with God. Be on guard against your children pitting the two of you against each other. Be united in your discipline, talking over parenting differences in private. And make it a mutual goal not to provoke your children. Your children will respond well to unity, gentleness, and thoughtfulness.

No role brings greater joy or blessing than being a parent. It is with love and a prayer for you that I share these principles that guided me during those active, hands-on, child-raising years:

- ⚘ love your husband
- ⚘ love your children
- ⚘ trust God for His strength
- ⚘ stand firm
- ⚘ own your responsibility
- ⚘ seek your husband's input
- ⚘ seek wise counsel from those who have gone before you
- ⚘ seek the Lord's wisdom through prayer and His Word

Lord, lead me to a deeper love and more patient under-standing for my family. As I study Your Word, guide me to be wise in my parenting. Help me follow Your design to be a worthy example to my family. Amen.

Living a Timothy Lifestyle

I trust in the Lord Jesus to send Timothy to you shortly,
that I also may be encouraged when I know your state. For
I have no one like-minded, who will sincerely care for your
state. For all seek their own, not the things which are of
Christ Jesus. But you know his proven character, that as a
son with his father he served with me in the gospel.

PHILIPPIANS 2:19-22

Have you ever said "Yes, but…"? It's amazing how one tiny word—*but*—can send such a strong signal of lack of faith or understanding. Do you contemplate the sacrifices made by Christ and think, "Yes, but that was *Jesus!* That was God in the flesh. I'm 'just' human."

Consider that Jesus thought of others all the time, He served people all the time (even when He was in prayer, it was to be refreshed so He could help us), and He submitted His will to His Father. Wouldn't it be great to be like that? "Yes, but…"

Well, the apostle Paul knew that a few of us might respond with that small but powerfully negative word. He introduces us to his assistant and traveling companion, Timothy, and says, "Okay, here's another person like me who thinks of others and not of himself." Timothy was "just" a human too. But he learned how to be a faithful servant. He grew that way because he was first a faithful student. May Timothy's example help you change your

"Yes, but…" to a "Yes, and I will…" There are no valid excuses to keep you from being a servant of the Lord.

How can you become more like Paul and Timothy in your service to the Lord and to the people around you?

- *Submit to God.* You are His servant.
- *Submit to another.* Perhaps to become a Timothy you need to submit to a Paul. Do you have someone you serve with shoulder-to-shoulder? Is there an older woman or another woman you help as she serves the Lord?
- *Mature in usefulness.* Sharpen your ministry skills and attitudes. Strengthen your faith. Increase your knowledge of the sacred Scriptures.
- *Be content to play second fiddle.* Harmony is produced in ministry when everyone seeks to be a servant.
- *Commit to "The Four A's."* Will you sign the statement below, which was presented at a conference I attended?

For You, Lord…

Anything
Anywhere
Any time
At any cost

_____   _____
Name   Date

What one behavior, heart concern, loyalty, or sacrifice drawn from the example of Timothy can you weave into your life of humble service to God's people?

Lord, help me serve side-by-side with others to bring glory to Your name through compassion and teaching and faithfulness. When I discount my potential as a servant because of my mistakes or lack of understanding, help me say yes to You and persevere. Amen.

Following Jesus

Jesus said to Simon, "Do not be afraid. From now on you
will catch men." So when they had brought their boats to
land, they forsook all and followed Him.

LUKE 5:10-11

As Jesus faithfully ministered to the multitudes, He was on
the lookout for people of passion and purpose, those willing to
make sacrifices to follow Him as their Master, those who would
count the cost and choose to follow Him. The crowds would
come, and eventually many would go. But in the ebb and flow of
the throng, a few would dedicate their lives to being with Jesus.

From Luke, you and I can learn what it means to *follow* Jesus.
One of the primary requirements is faith. We witness faith in
these people Jesus encounters.

The four fishermen—When Jesus performs a miracle by filling
the fishermen's nets with fish, they are astonished and don't feel
worthy of His presence. But when Jesus tells them that they will
now catch men, Simon Peter, James and John (sons of Zebedee),
and Andrew do not hesitate. They follow Jesus, leaving everything
they have known behind (Matthew 4; Luke 5). Have you made
following Jesus your first priority?

The leper—A leper falls to the ground and cries with absolute
faith in Jesus' power, "Lord, if You are willing, You can make

me clean" (Luke 5:12). Do you ask of Jesus with such conviction and belief?

The paralytic and his friends—A paralyzed man is lowered through the roof of a house by friends so he can be healed by Jesus. "When He saw their faith, He said to him, 'Man, your sins are forgiven you'" (Luke 5:20). Their determination revealed their faith. Will you do anything that is required of you to follow Jesus?

Aren't these amazing stories of faith? Do others witness the same passion and selflessness in your pursuit of Jesus and all that He calls you to be?

From God's Word to Your Heart

Christians love to sing about following Jesus. But following the Lord is no easy task or light commitment. Jesus is a loving-but-demanding Master. He expects His followers to listen, learn, and obey. When Jesus taught about being the bread of life, many fair-weather followers left. They could not accept His teaching (John 6:48-66).

Are you one who hesitates? Or do you say along with Peter, "Lord, to whom shall we go? You have the words of eternal life" (John 6:68). To live with passion and purpose you must follow Jesus wholeheartedly.

Do you know someone who needs to hear about Jesus? Be prayerful as you make plans to share the good news of the gospel.

Lord, You have called me, and I'm ready to follow. Help me be a witness of faith and passion as I share You with the people around me. Amen.

Waging Spiritual War

This charge I commit to you, son Timothy, according to the
prophecies previously made concerning you, that by them
you may wage the good warfare,
having faith and a good conscience.

1 Timothy 1:18

I'm not really a football fan, but after growing up with three
brothers and my dad, living with my husband, Jim, and having
two sons-in-law, I'm somewhat familiar with the game. You are
probably familiar with the game to some extent too. When the
players on a team gather in a circle during a game, this is called
a huddle. That's when the players are told what the play will be.

Well, today I want you to imagine such a huddle...a huddle
of two. The pair is made up of a seasoned coach—the apostle
Paul—and a young player—timid Timothy. Perhaps with his
arm affectionately around the young Timothy's shoulders, the
aged Paul gives his protégé a few words of exhortation on how
to handle the battles he's encountering at Ephesus.

How about you, my friend? Do you need some encouragement
today? Do you need a little advice for handling your difficult
situations? Like many good coaches, Paul uses images to help
explain to Timothy his position on the team.

A Christian must be a good soldier. Paul encouraged Timothy to "wage the good warfare" (verse 18). Paul isn't referring to a single battle but to a military campaign. Like Timothy, we too must...

- maintain a hold on faith and a good conscience
- cling tightly to our faith
- refuse to give in to temptation
- live out our faith with a clear conscience

A Christian must be a good sailor. In 1 Timothy 1:19, Paul switches from the picture of a military campaign to that of a shipwreck. What will help you and me navigate through sin and error? A good conscience—one that is guided by these forces:

- God's Word
- prayer
- Christian fellowship

From God's Word to Your Heart

The Christian life is a battle—a *spiritual* battle. We may not like it, and we may wish otherwise, but it's true. Therefore we, like Paul and Timothy, must fight the good fight. We must cling to two inseparable, valuable, dispositions of the heart—faith and a good conscience.

Is the Holy Spirit sounding any warning to your conscience about some aspect of your behavior? Are you doing what you know is right in every area of your life? Or are you deliberately ignoring an inner tug? Take some time to reflect on these tough-but-important questions. Huddle with God and ask Him for the game plan. Heed His wisdom and instruction. When you fumble, when you drop the ball (and it will happen), God has given you a way back to His plan: "If we confess our sins, He is faithful and just to forgive us our sins and to cleanse us from all unrighteousness" (1 John 1:9).

And then accept God's forgiveness and grace and get back into the game.

> *Lord, You know I need Your guidance and instruction daily. I confess my sins to You today so that I can continue in Your plan. Please lead me through the battle to victory. Amen.*

Thinking of Others

That you also may know my affairs and
how I am doing, Tychicus, a beloved brother and
faithful minister in the Lord, will make
all things known to you; whom I have
sent to you for this very purpose, that you
may know our affairs, and that
he may comfort your hearts.

EPHESIANS 6:21-22

Don't you just love to receive a "Thinking of you" greeting card? I purchased a package of cards to keep on hand for encouraging those I know who are downhearted or suffering in some way.

Even though he is suffering in prison, the apostle Paul writes an encouraging letter to the believers in Ephesus meant to be read in all the churches in the region. He chooses to send the note via the hands of a trusted friend, who will take Paul's personal greetings to the people and update them on how he is doing.

Are you thinking of others today? Even if you're facing difficult circumstances, you can share your heart with people by focusing on the blessings that come to you from God the Father and your Lord Jesus Christ, including:

❧ *peace* in your life circumstances

- *love* that is unconditional and constant
- *faith* that is strong and unswerving
- *grace* and myriad other blessings

Speaking from my own heart, it's been a wonderful experience becoming better acquainted with some of the many and marvelous blessings that are ours in Christ Jesus...blessings from the very heights of heaven. It's incredible to realize that as children and daughters of the King, you and I have received *every spiritual blessing* (Ephesians 1:3). Believe it because God says it! This fact alone should prompt us to fall to our knees in adoring praise.

My friend, as you are obedient to God and rely on the power of the Spirit, you will experience the daily reality of your heavenly blessings in Christ.

> *Lord, help me to think of others and to share Your love with them so they too can experience the countless blessings You give. May I hold tightly to Your promises and the great gifts of your peace, love, and grace. Amen.*

Counting on God's Grace and Peace

Grace to you and peace be multiplied.

1 PETER 1:2

You're a special woman. I know it. Do you know how I know? You're pursuing grace and peace by spending time in these devotions and in God's Word. When God lives within us, His Spirit causes us to yearn for a gentle calm in our lives.

Are you struggling or suffering? Are you facing a painful loss? A common response women have when they're first asked to contemplate a gentle and quiet spirit is to declare, "But I can't be like that. I can't remain calm when there's trouble." True...if we're relying on our own strength. But when we appropriate God's great enablers—His grace and His peace—we can achieve gentleness and calmness even during hard times. We just need to...

- *count on God's grace.* It's given. It's here. It's available.
- *pray for God's grace.* Your awareness of God's grace will expand when you give more things and more of you to Him.
- *get on with life.* Regardless of our struggles, it's possible—and important—to have something positive to show for our suffering, including how much God loves us, cares for us, and provides for us.

It's wonderful to think about God's grace and peace. They are two of the loveliest gifts He bestows on us. The very words move our souls.

Grace is active and means "favor." So whatever your situation, whatever the occasion, you have God's favor. You have what you need to endure, cope, and have victory. Peter prays that God's grace will be with the people he's writing to...including you and me.

Peace, on the other hand, is passive and refers to rest. And so, dear one, whatever your situation, whatever the occasion or need, you have God's peace. You have God's rest *in* your suffering.

Yes, as we suffer for doing what's right and are enabled by the power of God's grace and enjoying His peace, as we put on God's gentle and quiet spirit and rely on the Lord instead of our human efforts and emotions, as we wait on Him to help us make sense of our suffering times, then indeed we have much to show in the end. Every time we endure hard times, we prove that the glory of the Lord is truly revealed in the end. As the psalmist declared, "Oh, taste and see that the LORD is good; blessed is the man [or woman] who trusts in Him!" (Psalm 34:8).

> *God, I cry out to You during this time of strife. Your grace and peace lead me to adopt a gentle and quiet spirit even now...especially now. I will trust in Your strength and not my own as I wait for Your healing and direction. Amen.*

Shining Lights

Do all things without murmuring and disputing, that
you may become blameless and harmless, children of
God without fault in the midst of a crooked and perverse
generation, among whom you shine as lights in the world,
holding fast the word of life, so that I may rejoice in the day
of Christ that I have not run in vain or labored in vain.

PHILIPPIANS 2:14-16

If you're a parent, you know parenting is always accompanied
by a multitude of hopes and prayers. With deep love for your
children, you bear down during the formative years to ensure
that values, training, and discipline are applied in ample measure.
Prayers are lifted daily for the ultimate outcome of your love and
labors: *Will they grow up to love the Lord? To follow God's ways?
To heed the Word of the Lord? To point others to the Savior?*

As Paul addresses his beloved children in the Lord at Philippi,
he also instructs us, like a parent, to fulfill the spiritual accomplishments that make our faith evident. Paul wants God's children
to shine as lights to the world. What wisdom is Paul sharing?

- Live out your salvation, carry it to its conclusion, and
  apply it to day-by-day living.
- Actively pursue obedience as God produces spiritual
  fruit in your life.

- Hold fast to the truths and principles in God's Word.
- Follow Christ's example by serving others to encourage them to become believers and grow in their faith.

Paul—our teacher and spiritual parent—longs for us to be strong, faithful, and obedient children of God.

From God's Word to Your Heart

After Dr. Louis Talbot's death, his wife, Dr. Carol Talbot, wrote a biography of her husband's life and entitled it *For This I Was Born*. I loved reading about the fascinating and inspiring life of this great saint, preacher, and founder of a seminary that bears his name. I especially love the title.

Do you know what your purpose is, dear one? Can you boldly declare, "For this I was born" and know what the "this" is? Jesus could! He clearly stated, "For this cause I was born" when He was questioned by Pilate (John 18:37). Jesus went on to say, "I have come into the world, that I should bear witness to the truth. Everyone who is of the truth hears My voice."

Are you living out your purpose for God's good pleasure without murmuring and disputing? Are you studying God's instructions and being obedient so you can discover your great purpose in Christ? You have been given the gift of being a child of God. Your heavenly Father wants to see you shine for Him. For this cause... for this privilege...you were born—to shine lights in the world.

Father, what a gift You've given me, Your child. Your Word is filled with Your instructions and guidance as my parent. You also blessed me with spiritual parents, including Paul, who encourage and inspire me to faithfully obey and model a heart committed to sacrifice and service. Thank You. Amen.

Handling Temptation

Jesus answered and said to [the devil], "It has been said,
'You shall not tempt the LORD your God.'"

LUKE 4:12

Have you heard someone shout "The devil made me do it!" when trying to explain away a sin or failure? Whether in jest or not, this is not exactly a true statement. In actuality, as one person quipped, "We start the fire, and the devil supplies the gasoline." Building the fire is our choice. In the opening verses of Luke 4, when the crafty devil was trying to entice Jesus, we see a different picture. Jesus never allowed the fire to start, which didn't give the devil the opportunity to pour gas on the fire! Note how Jesus was tested, fought the battle, handled temptation, won the victory, and went on in the power of the Holy Spirit to mightily teach the truth and wondrously display His authority.

The devil said to Him, "If You are the Son of God, command this stone to become bread."

But Jesus answered him, saying, "It is written, 'Man shall not live by bread alone, but by every word of God'" (verses 3 and 4).

Then the devil, taking Him up on a high mountain, showed Him all the kingdoms of the world in a moment of time.

And the devil said to Him, "All this authority I will give You…if You will worship before me…"

And Jesus answered and said to him, "Get behind Me, Satan! For it is written, 'You shall worship the Lord your God, and Him only you shall serve'" (verses 5-8).

Then [the devil] brought [Jesus] to Jerusalem, set Him on the pinnacle of the temple, and said to Him, "If You are the Son of God, throw Yourself down from here. For it is written: 'He shall give His angels charge over you…'"

And Jesus answered and said to him, "It has been said, 'You shall not tempt the Lord your God'" (verses 9-10,12).

Jesus rebuked Satan and every temptation. We can resist temptation as we turn to the power of Christ found in the truths of Scripture. So what can you do the next time you are tested?

Trust that God is faithful. He will not "allow you to be tempted beyond what you are able, but with the temptation will also make the way of escape, that you may be able to bear it" (1 Corinthians 10:13).

Take up the whole armor of God. If you gird your waist with truth, don the breastplate of righteousness, put on the shoes of the gospel of peace, grip the shield of faith, wear the helmet of salvation, and wield the sword of the Spirit (God's Word), you are ready for battle (Ephesians 6:13-17).

Know you are not alone in your trial. Our High Priest, Jesus Christ, was tempted as you are. He is compassionate and understanding of what you face. He won't leave you alone in your trial. You can go "boldly to the throne of grace, that [you] may obtain mercy and find grace to help in time of need" (Hebrews 4:16). Jesus stands ready to help you!

Having a purpose, a goal, is one of the most dynamic forces in human nature. With purpose, a man or woman can accomplish amazing feats, achieve challenging goals, and persist through staggering difficulties. Without purpose, many people drift through life with little to show for their existence.

Do you know your purpose? Your reason for being? The course of your day at each fresh sunrise? Joshua knew his. He declared, "As for me and my house, we will serve the LORD" (Joshua 24:15). Mary, the mother of Jesus, knew her purpose. She said, "Behold the maidservant of the Lord! Let it be to me according to your word" (Luke 1:38). Paul knew his purpose. He proclaimed, "For to me, to live is Christ" (Philippians 1:21). If you're unsure of your purpose, ask God and others to help you understand. Then you can focus on living for Christ and doing what He wants you to do. And remember, with God's help you can handle temptation and stay on target.

God, I come before Your throne today knowing that in this life I'll face temptations that could threaten me and my faith. Remind me to turn to Your Word and put on the full armor You provide so I'll be protected and victorious. Thank You for Your mercy and faithfulness. Amen.

Recognizing False Teachers

If anyone teaches [a different doctrine] and does not consent
to wholesome words, even the words of our Lord Jesus Christ,
and to the doctrine which accords with godliness, he is proud,
knowing nothing, but is obsessed with disputes and arguments
over words, from which come envy, strife, reviling, evil suspicions,
useless wranglings of men of corrupt minds and destitute of the
truth, who suppose that godliness is a means of gain.
From such withdraw yourself.

1 Timothy 6:3-5

My friend, I have great news about the good news. The Bible
contains *everything* we need for life and godliness! God has packed
in a multitude of subjects. When we see a teaching principle
repeated, we know God wants us to pay close attention. So sit
up and take note today. Paul is repeating—for the third time—
instructions concerning recognizing false teachers. Let's pay special
attention to three marks of a false teacher.

Different doctrine. False teachers promote principles that don't
agree with Paul's teachings, and, consequently, Jesus' teachings.
How can you know false teaching? By studying Scripture! The
more you know, the better you'll be at identifying errors.

Pride. Pride has been at the root of most of humankind's
problems. It can infect any of us in a variety of ways: wealth,
possessions, education, knowledge, privilege, even humility.

Controversy-rousing speech. Words can have powerful effects. The words of a false teacher bring forth the fruits of controversy, strife, useless disputes, and fighting over what truth is. You and I are called to speak wholesome words, healthy words, profitable words. Our words should build up, edify, and encourage people.

From God's Word to Your Heart

Do you yearn to live a godly life...a holy life? One vital step is increasing your knowledge and understanding of God's Word. Psalm 19:7-9 notes:

The law of the LORD is perfect, converting the soul;

The testimony of the LORD is sure, making wise the simple;

The statutes of the LORD are right, rejoicing the heart;

The commandment of the LORD is pure, enlightening the eyes;

The fear of the LORD is clean, enduring forever;

The judgments of the LORD are true and righteous altogether.

In Ephesians 4:29 Paul instructs us to "let no corrupt word proceed out of your mouth, but what is good for necessary edification, that it may impart grace to the hearers." How are you doing in this regard? Do you make the effort to speak wholesome, gracious words of health and encouragement? Do you recognize false teachings and teach the truth? Are there changes you need to make in your speech and attitude? And what part will God's Word play in your plan for pursuing godliness?

> *Lord, may my words be wholesome and profitable. May I hold tightly to the words of Jesus as truth so that I never teach false doctrines. I want to communicate Your truth and Your way. Amen.*

Preparing for Warfare

Be strong in the Lord and in the power of His might.

EPHESIANS 6:10

You are the recipient of many spiritual blessings, and God gives you plenty of opportunities to serve Him and be a blessing to others. But the call to live a Spirit-controlled life isn't always blissful. Ephesians 6 tells us to be strong in the Lord and call on His might because we will be doing battle "against principalities, against powers, against the rulers of the darkness of this age, against spiritual hosts of wickedness" (verse 12).

Is your first thought the same as mine? *Didn't I sign up for love, not war?* Isn't being a Christian all about focusing on God's grace and mercy and love? The apostle Paul reminds us that our strong faith in God places us on Satan's hit list. A woman who loves God and serves His people is a threat to the devil, and he will do everything possible to get our focus off following Christ.

From God's Word to Your Heart

There are plenty of battles in our day-to-day physical lives. Battle of the bulge, battle with children to get them to eat vegetables, the battle to pay the bills, the battle to...well, you know the list can go on and on! But you and I—and all believers—need to recognize why we are usually unprepared for the spiritual battle.

- *We don't recognize the danger.* We consistently underestimate the power of Satan.
- *We don't understand the importance of the armor God provides.* Good news! God's Word (Ephesians, chapter 6, specifically) reveals how to get dressed for battle.
- *We don't take to heart the fact that we're in a spiritual battle.* Without preparation and training, no soldier is ready for battle…including us.
- *We fail to realize we are constantly in a battle zone.* We're not merely in a mall, or an office, or a school, or even a house or apartment. Everywhere we go is part of Satan's territory, so we'd better be aware of it so we can be ready, willing, and able to fight.

God doesn't leave us defenseless! Turning to the truth of His Word, we can become spiritually prepared to fight and win the war. War sounds intimidating, doesn't it? That's why we don't take on spiritual opponents in our own strength. No, we rest fully in the strength of the Lord and the power of His might.

Victory is yours in Jesus Christ. Ask God to give you the resolve to "take up the whole armor of God, that you may be able to withstand in the evil day, and having done all, to stand" (Ephesians 6:13). When you are victorious on this front, the battles you experience at home, work, and in relationships are put into perspective and often resolved.

> *Father, show me the way into battle. When I focus so much on daily human battles, I often forget to be on guard against the spiritual battle. Protect me from the enemy's tactics. Give me Your wisdom as I prepare and Your strength and might and wisdom so I can be victorious and glorify You. Amen.*

Defining True Wisdom

The wisdom that is from above is first pure,
then peaceable, gentle, willing to yield, full of mercy
and good fruits, without partiality and without hypocrisy.
Now the fruit of righteousness is sown in peace by
those who make peace.

JAMES 3:17-18

A life of lovely graciousness models the fruit of wisdom and its rare fragrances of humility and gentleness. We can tell a lot about a person's faith life by how well she sows wisdom and peace. The world judges beauty by external elements: the style of a woman's hair, the designer labels on her clothes, the monetary value of her house and car. But God's beauty pours forth in the form of edifying godly words of wisdom that bring blessings to its hearers.

Consider these definitions and explanations of the eight components James shares on spiritual wisdom, the kind that comes down from above.

- *Pure*—True wisdom is free from ulterior motives and self-interest.
- *Peaceable*—True wisdom accomplishes peace in our relationships with others and with God.
- *Gentle*—True wisdom offers forgiveness and extends kindness and consideration to everyone.

- *Willing to yield*—True wisdom is marked by a willingness to listen and a sense of knowing when to yield.
- *Full of mercy*—True wisdom reaches out to help others.
- *Full of good fruits*—True wisdom bears "good fruits" of action.
- *Without partiality*—True wisdom does not waver or vacillate in indecision or play favorites in dispensing truth and holding to its standard.
- *Without hypocrisy*—True wisdom does not deal in deception, pretension, or selfishness.

From God's Word to Your Heart

How did you do with the checklist? Are these "good fruits" evident in your life? Did you find any of these marks of wisdom missing from your lips and your ways? Think a moment about your relationships and your effect on others. Are you a promoter of peace and righteousness?

May yours be a heart of wisdom! And may your words be filled with God's wisdom. And may your prayer be a humble request to never put yourself or your opinions above the needs of others. Become that sower of peace in your family. Speak words of mercy and be sincere in your forgiveness of others. You'll experience the gracious beauty of a life overflowing with true wisdom—God's wisdom.

God, when I rely on my wisdom and the influences of the world, I end up sowing discontent and jealousy. I don't want to rely on my emotions or the trends of the season. I want my life to bear the fruit of Your wisdom so I bring blessings to others and praise to Your name. Amen.

Living in the Presence of God

He indeed was foreordained before the foundation of
the world, but was manifest in these last times for
you who through Him believe in God, who raised Him
from the dead and gave Him glory, so that your faith
and hope are in God.

1 Peter 1:20-21

What does your salvation mean to you? What difference does
it make in your daily life to know that Jesus laid down His life
and shed His precious blood for you? Let's look at two saints who
gave these facts some thought and then promptly made serious
changes in their lives. The first is Jenny Lind, a spectacular singer
in the early 1800s who was known as "The Swedish Nightingale."
When Miss Lind was asked why she abandoned the stage at the
very height of her success, she replied with her finger on a Bible,
"When every day it made me think less of this, what could I do?"

The second person is a captain in the Army in the same era
as Miss Lind. The story is told that Hedley Vicars sat in a hotel
room awaiting the arrival of another officer. He idly turned the
pages of the Bible. His eye alighted on these words: "The blood
of Jesus Christ his Son cleanseth us from all sin" (1 John 1:7 kjv).
Closing the Book, he vowed, "If this is true for me, henceforth
I will live, by the grace of God, as a man who has been washed
in the blood of Christ."

The awesome facts of Jesus' death *for* you should make every difference *to* you! God's presence and the truth of your salvation should inspire you to...

- live a life of holiness, striving to be set apart for God
- live a life of fear, being in awe of God's might and mercy
- live a life transformed by God's grace
- live as a prisoner who has been set free and praises her emancipator

From God's Word to Your Heart

In the quiet of spending time in the truth of God's Word, ask, "Am I continuing to turn my back on my former life? Have I soberly acknowledged that God is a judge and will judge me according to my deeds? Am I living my life in healthy reverential fear, not as one who's afraid of God, but as one who respects and reveres the all-powerful Creator?"

I know you don't want to offend God or take Him for granted. So keep checking your attitudes and behaviors. Have you broken from your life before Christ? Have you taken on new behaviors—the behaviors of one redeemed by the precious blood of the spotless Jesus? As great as the depth of your sinfulness is, the height of God's redeeming love is always more than enough. Live daily with that fact in mind...and an overwhelming love for Jesus in your heart.

> *Lord, I'm so thankful for the gift of salvation and for Your presence in my life every day. May my daily life reflect Your presence and my gratitude to You. Keep me from returning to the ways of my past. I want my intentions and actions to always be pleasing in Your sight. Amen.*

Looking to the Needs of Others

Let nothing be done through selfish ambition or conceit,
but in lowliness of mind let each esteem others better than himself.
Let each of you look out not only for his own interests, but also
for the interests of others.

PHILIPPIANS 2:3-4

For several years my husband's office door at The Master's Seminary displayed a cartoon that depicted the expectations of many people who attend church regularly. As the preacher in the picture prepared to preach, he faced his congregation. Those sitting in front of him wore expectant expressions, and their thoughts were verbalized in the familiar bubble format above each head. One by one their thoughts were: "Feed me!" "Encourage me!" "Teach me!" "Lead me!" "Comfort me!" "Disciple me!" "Support me!" Each person present had "needs," and each person expected their pastor to meet all of those needs.

Today's passage shines light on our "needs" and shows us how these needs are truly met. Every Christian has been given consolation in Christ—the comfort of love, the fellowship of the Spirit, and God's affection and mercy. We are well loved! This enables us to point away from ourselves and concentrate on meeting the needs of others. When we care for one another, we are helping to meet the needs of the body of Christ.

When I think of "lowliness of mind" (see verse 3), I can't help but think of flowers. The more mature they are and the bigger their blossoms, the more their heads bow. I so enjoy the delightful perfumes made from their crushed blossoms. What inspiring pictures of humility.

While we may desire the exquisite grace of humility, how is such beauty realized? How can we nurture a heart of humility? Here are a few scriptural guidelines.

- *Know yourself.* We are made in the image of God, but we are also sinners in need of a renewed mind so we'll think properly about ourselves.

- *Respect others.* Jesus told His disciples to major on service to others. He "did not come to be served, but to serve, and to give His life a ransom for many" (Mark 10:45). Indeed, as Paul exhorts, we are to consider others to be better than ourselves.

- *Pray faithfully.* Everything about prayer is humbling—from its posture to its petitions. In prayer we bow humbly before God Almighty, confess our sins, praise our heavenly Father for all He has done for us, and ask for His mercy on us and on others.

- *Imitate Christ's humility.* This, dear one, is the key to lowliness of mind.

Don't become someone who always depends on her pastor (or someone else) to meet your needs. Look to Christ! He's your answer for everything you need. Then turn your attention to the needs of others and minister with a humble, grateful heart.

Lord, I bow before You with a humble heart and spirit. I'm so grateful for the assurance of Your comfort and care. I rest in You. Lead me so I'll see the needs of those around me and actively serve the body of Christ. Amen.

Loving Money

For the love of money is a root of all kinds of evil, for
which some have strayed from the faith in
their greediness, and pierced themselves
through with many sorrows.

1 Timothy 6:10

News flash! We are money managers whether we have paying jobs or not and whether we're married or not. We manage our households on a budget. We save money. And we give our money to others. To add to our list of principles and precepts regarding finances, Paul gets to the heart of the matter and addresses "the love of money." Have you invested in the following truths?

Our value is in God. When we are godly and content as righteous believers, we have our gain and our worth. Looking for worldly sources of affluence will destroy our godly desires. Let's keep our eyes on where our value lies.

The love of money is evil. Some misquote Paul and say, "Money is the root of all evil," but notice that Paul says "the *love* of money" is a root of all kinds of evil. There's no problem working for money and providing for the necessities. The problem comes with misplaced *desire* and misplaced affection.

Lust destroys godly priorities. When we crave riches, we fall prey to temptations and to prideful desires. Lust shifts our hearts from being godly to being self-serving. A person with a lustful heart is never satisfied because she strays from godliness and the contentment of living in her value as a child of God.

From God's Word to Your Heart

Look in your heart. What do you require for contentment? Are food and clothing and shelter enough? Do you desire more than is needed when you shop, receive, gather, and plan? Thank God for His abundant provision for your necessities...your *true* necessities.

The Proverbs 31 woman reveals a godly balance in the area of money. Her motives were *pure*—she desired to help and to better her family. And her motives were *godly*—she gave her money to the poor and needy, assisting her community.

The best way to guard against the love of money is to be a "generous soul" (Proverbs 11:25). Who needs your money today? What missionary ministry could be bettered by a contribution from you? How could your church benefit from your liberality? Why not make a contribution to help the poor and needy in your community? Ask God to guide you with His beautiful grace of giving.

> *Lord, keep me from loving money. Help me become a generous giver to Your church and to Your children near and far. Protect me from the love of money. I rest in my value in You. Thank You for giving me contentment. Amen.*

Learning How to Live

Blessed are you poor, for yours is the kingdom of God. Blessed
are you who hunger now, for you shall be filled.

LUKE 6:20-21

Is your "to do" list like mine...longer than the day ahead? Well,
Jesus has a message for us! In His perfect wisdom, He shows us
the value of foresight, prayer, preparation, and priorities when
making sure what is truly important gets done.

In the book of Luke, we see that Jesus' ministry was, by human
standards, a success—crowds, followers, and a number of faithful
disciples. But our Lord knew time was growing short. In a few
months He would set His face toward Jerusalem and the cross.
Who would continue His ministry after He was gone? After praying all night, Jesus shifted the focus of His time and ministry. He
selected 12 men to personally train—men who would later be
sent forth as His apostles. We are blessed with the opportunity
to learn the lessons Jesus taught His new ambassadors on how
to live in a new world order, in the kingdom of God.

- *Love your enemies.* "And just as you want men to do to
  you, you also do to them likewise" (Luke 6:31).

- *Do not judge.* "Judge not, and you shall not be judged...
  Forgive, and you will be forgiven" (verse 37).

- *A life is known by its fruit.* "A good man out of the good treasure of his heart brings forth good" (verse 45).

- *Build on the truth.* "Whoever comes to Me, and hears My sayings and does them, I will show you whom he is like: He is like a man building a house, who dug deep and laid the foundation on the rock" (verses 47-48).

From God's Word to Your Heart

If you've read the four Gospels in the New Testament, you no doubt know of Jesus' famous Sermon on the Mount. In fact, some have asked, "Are the teachings of Jesus in Luke 6:20-49 part of that well-loved sermon?" While Luke's presentation contains similarities to the full sermon recorded in Matthew, chapters 5 through 7, it is also possible that, like all good teachers, Jesus may have given similar teachings on various occasions.

But whether Luke's information was part of the better-known sermon or not, the important thing is that the apostles were the recipients of Jesus' teaching. These men were being groomed by the Lord for a worldwide ministry. They needed to glimpse and grasp their purpose so that one day, when the time was right, their Holy Spirit-infused passion would thrust them into a fearless ministry of boldly proclaiming the good news of the risen Savior. Are you ready to live God's way? Pray for God's vision and priorities for your life today. Then live it!

Lord, I love Your ways. I walk in them with a heart of gratitude. I pray that the fruit of my life will show others my passion for Your truth and purpose. Amen.

God's Design for Marriage

Just as the church is subject to Christ, so let the wives
be to their own husbands in everything. Husbands,
love your wives, just as Christ also loved the church
and gave Himself for her.

EPHESIANS 5:24-25

Marriage is not man's invention. No, it was God's idea. In fact, marriage was the first institution God established after creating Adam and Eve. In them He formed the perfect team. They were to be a unified and indivisible force. However, with the entrance of sin into the world, that team became fractured as each brought self-interest into the marriage.

When Paul addressed the Ephesians about the importance of being filled with the Holy Spirit in the marriage relationship, it was revolutionary information…and it still is revolutionary! God's Word gives us radical and miracle-working advice.

- *Wives submit to husbands.* We are called to follow—to submit to and respect—our husbands. As Christians we are to voluntarily arrange ourselves under one another as God commands…not over one another.

- *Husbands submit to Christ's example.* Our husbands are to love us with the same love Christ has for His church.

A marriage with this unconditional love experiences the depth of grace and mercy.

⯈ *Everyone submits to one another.* Being in a godly marriage provides us with a practical, influential example of how to respect and serve everyone in our lives.

From God's Word to Your Heart

Marriage is often described as the union of two selfish sinners. Therein lies the problem! God didn't intend for the marriage relationship to be this way. The fall of man into sin affected everything and every relationship, including marriage. That's a true picture of paradise lost. But God has provided a solution for struggles in marriage—Jesus Christ. Ah, paradise regained!

You can't make your husband love you, but you can do your part by loving your husband using the biblical pattern of submission and respect. The next time your sin nature tugs at you to disrespect your husband, think of your Lord. Jesus willingly submitted to the Father's will because of His love for the Father. God is asking you to respect and submit to your husband out of love and respect for Him. If you obey God's plan and follow Christ's example, you will be following God's design for your marriage. And it's a perfect design!

Lord, help me line up under Your command so my marriage can be all that You designed it to be. Thank You, Jesus, for giving me Your example of love and respect so I can enjoy the goodness of a healthy relationship. Amen.

Loving One Another

Since you have purified your souls in
obeying the truth through the Spirit in sincere
love of the brethren, love one another
fervently with a pure heart.

1 PETER 1:22

How does your life garden grow? Does it produce the fruit of the Spirit listed in Galatians 5:22-23? God grows these nine qualities—love, joy, peace, longsuffering, kindness, goodness, faithfulness, gentleness, self-control—in our lives when we are abiding in Him and walking with Him by His Spirit.

And what is the first quality that life in Christ should manifest in us? *Love.* Your salvation in Christ first makes a transforming impression on how you live your life, and then it makes a big difference in your relationships with others. How? Through *love.* And how are we to love people?

Sincerely. We're not to merely express love verbally and in gushy terms, but we're to genuinely love one another. As the apostle John wrote, "Let us not love in word or in tongue, but in deed and in truth" (1 John 3:18). Sincere love holds no grudges. Sincere love doesn't ask or expect anything in return. Are you ever less than sincere with your love?

Fervently. We are to love with an intense love, a stretched-to-the-furthest-point love. Our love is to be limitless. We're to withhold nothing. This is not a warm and fuzzy kind of love. It's all-out and total. Do you love with gusto?

Heartily. A mighty, meaningful love comes *from* the heart and is lived out *with* the heart. We are to love one another with all our hearts and with all our strength. Yes, love truly is a matter of the heart. How are you measuring up?

From God's Word to Your Heart

It's easy to see that the kind of love God calls us to exhibit—sincere, fervent, and hearty—will cost us greatly and require much effort, isn't it? It may even include suffering. And if that happens, we're to put on God's gentle and quiet spirit to endure any ill treatment and still give love in return. Remember that a gentle spirit doesn't cause disturbances…and doesn't react to the disturbances caused by others. Instead we love—earnestly, genuinely, and wholeheartedly—even those who cause us to suffer. As one person observed, "Wherever you find love, you find self-denial."

This message from God regarding your love life is life-changing…and life-challenging! But you can do it! Extend the love God gives to you to others. The love that God demonstrated toward you—while you were unlovely and a vile sinner—turn around and demonstrate toward others—even those who are unlovely and vile. It's easy to talk about how much you love God, but loving others reveals how much you truly do. It's a supernatural display of God in you. Where love resides, God abides.

God, give me Your heart for others so that I love others
with a sincere, fervent, and hearty love. Amen.

Planning with Wisdom

If the Lord wills, we shall live and do this or that.

JAMES 4:15

Are you a planner? Do you have a life-management system for organizing your time so you can accomplish what you must... and maybe a little more? Most of the women I know have some sort of notebook set up to organize their tasks and roles and responsibilities as busy women with people to serve and work to accomplish. I have such a planner (actually, more than one!) for my days, my family, my home, my projects, my relationships, and my ministries.

Whatever system we use, it's important to carry out our management and planning with *divine style.* How are you when it comes to including God in your planning sessions? Do you pray over your schedules? When you speak of the future—even the next hour—do you add to your thoughts and words "Lord willing" or "If the Lord wills"? I'm sure you don't want to commit a sin of omission—of not including God when you plan.

From God's Word to Your Heart

There are two conditions we should be careful not to violate in our decision making and planning. The first is failing to consider our finiteness as humans. Let's face it—our knowledge is limited. We have no way of knowing what the future holds for us. The second is failing to consider the uncertainty of life, which James describes as a vapor (James 5:14).

What is the pattern of your life? Are you a "doer of the Word"? When you discover new counsel from the Lord, do you leap immediately into action, ensuring that you incorporate what you've learned, making your new knowledge about God's will part of your life? Or do you wait, hanging on to a few favorite sins, before you relinquish them and do the right thing? As writer Elisabeth Elliot noted, "Delayed obedience is disobedience."

As a woman after God's own heart who desires to grow in wisdom and plan in wisdom, follow these basic principles:

- Realize only God knows your future.
- Realize God has a purpose for your life.
- Realize God may send interruptions into your "perfect" day.
- Remember to pray over your plans, asking God for guidance.
- Remember to say, "If the Lord wills…"

Being a good steward of your time is important. And since you don't know what the future holds, stay flexible and be open to what God has in mind. Although you don't know the future, you do know the One who manages the past, the present, and the future! Ask God, "What's next?"

> *God, You are the only One who knows what tomorrow will bring. Help me plan my day and my week with wisdom. As I take steps forward to make the most of each day, guide me and remind me to be open to any unexpected turns You might bring my way. Amen.*

Praying for Others

And this I pray, that your love may abound still more and
more in knowledge and all discernment, that you may approve
the things that are excellent, that you may be sincere and
without offense till the day of Christ, being filled with the
fruits of righteousness which are by Jesus Christ,
to the glory and praise of God.

Philippians 1:9-11

Every Christian prays for those she loves and cares about. Yet it's easy to fall into a pattern of praying for the temporal things in the lives of those we cherish. It doesn't take much thought to ask God to bless people financially or to resolve their health concerns. We can soon find ourselves praying in a routine sort of way for family and friends looking for places to live, selecting colleges, or seeking jobs. Then there are our habitual prayers for the daily little things in life—parking places, bargains, our children to nap well, safety for one more day.

God's faithful servant Paul shows us a more significant way to pray for those we know and love. It's far from what could be called a "baby prayer"—a prayer for health, wealth, and happiness. Paul prays an "adult prayer" for his beloved friends—a prayer for spiritual knowledge and discernment, sincerity and integrity, acceptance of what is godly and holy, and lives filled with righteousness. And by the way, these are not just topics to cover in your prayers for others. These are mature issues to lift up for yourself too.

And this I pray, dear friend and sister in Christ, for you and me:

- ☞ I pray that we learn the discipline of lifting our thoughts and our prayers, our aims and our lives, heavenward, upward, far above and beyond that which is routine and mundane.
- ☞ I pray that we become stronger women of prayer—with regular, daily, unhurried, secret lingering in prayer.
- ☞ I pray that others will be encouraged by knowing we pray for them…and by knowing *what* we pray for them.
- ☞ I pray we will pray as Paul did, using the sweet-but-packed wisdom found in Philippians 1:9-11 as our guide to praying for others.
- ☞ I pray our lives will bring great glory and praise to our Lord Jesus Christ and God, our Father; that our lives will be filled with the fruits of righteousness.
- ☞ I pray that the fruit in our lives will be abundant and spill forth, blessing others and reflecting well on our Savior.

God, lead my focus away from temporal items. Give me a vision for those things that are eternal and of spiritual importance. And when I pray for others, help me be sincere and faithful. Amen.

Watching Out for False Teachers

Some, having strayed, have turned aside to idle talk,
desiring to be teachers of the law, understanding
neither what they say nor the things which they affirm.

1 TIMOTHY 1:6-7

One of my favorite descriptions and pictures of the Proverbs 31 woman is that of her *watching* over her family and home: "She *watches* over the ways of her household" (verse 27). As wives and mothers and homemakers, we wear many hats as we discharge our duties at home. And there's no doubt that one of our most important duties is that of a "watchwoman." Just as the walls of the ancient cities were dotted with watchmen who guarded the towns 24 hours a day against hostile action, we too faithfully and carefully guard our children from harmful influences and sound a warning to our husbands when we feel the family is threatened.

Paul watched too. He checked on and encouraged the people who attended the churches under his charge. In fact, when Paul listed his sufferings for the cause of Christ, he ended his list by stating that "besides the other things, what comes upon me daily: my deep concern for all the churches" (2 Corinthians 11:28). He worried about false teachers promoting ungodliness.

As we pray against the ungodly influences that could cast darkness over our families, our children, and our hearts, what can we watch for? Look for three bright stars produced by sound, biblical teaching:

- ✷ *Godly edification*—Sound teaching furthers the plan of God (1 Timothy 1:4).
- ✷ *Good fruit*—Sound teaching comes from the heart of a sincere teacher (verse 5).
- ✷ *Glorious gospel*—Sound teaching showcases the glory of God (verse 11).

You are this woman—the one who watches over her home and family with a prayerful heart.

From God's Word to Your Heart

Don't you want to learn and grow so you can understand the doctrines of the Christian faith better? So you can teach them to your children and help others? You can start by studying the Bible, attending Bible-study classes, and memorizing Scripture. The more you know, the more effective your protection of your loved ones will be. How can you not be fooled by false teaching? Answer: By being familiar with the truth! Put W-A-T-C-H to work in your life today:

> **W**ant to be with God's people
> **A**sk God for discernment
> **T**ake in God's Word
> **C**arefully select a Bible-teaching church
> **H**eed the warnings of Scripture

Keep watch over your spiritual well-being so you can help your family and friends distinguish light from dark.

Lord, my attention gets caught up in daily needs and tasks so easily. Paul reminds me to scan the horizon and pay attention to the influences around my family and me. Give me a heart of discernment so I can watch for those who teach Your light and avoid those who don't. Amen.

Practicing Wise Living

Do not be unwise, but understand
what the will of the Lord is.

EPHESIANS 5:17

"Make a wish!" How often have you said or heard this statement on your birthday or one of your children's birthdays before blowing out candles on a cake? God, in essence, made a similar statement to King Solomon thousands of years ago. In fact, God told Solomon he could have anything he wanted. *Anything!* That's right. Let's see...how about a new car, a new house, new clothes, new... You probably know this story found in 1 Kings 3. What did Solomon ask for? Wisdom! He asked for "an understanding heart to judge Your people, that I may discern between good and evil" (verse 9). The next time you pray or "make a wish" (so to speak), follow Solomon's example. Don't waste your breath on physical or earthly desires and needs. Instead, go for the biggest and best of all: wisdom.

As a believer infused with the light of Christ, you have His wisdom and prudence. So the question isn't "Do I have wisdom?" but "How do I apply the wisdom and discretion I've been given?" Can these attributes be found in your life?

> *Wisdom walks carefully.* Are you meticulously careful about the life you lead? Keep your mind on God's Word and watch over your lifestyle so you'll walk with God.

- *Wisdom evaluates its time.* The time you have in this life is so brief. Don't let it be stolen by uselessness. Instead, make every minute count for eternity.
- *Wisdom follows a standard.* God's standards are revealed in His Word. Isn't it exciting to witness His plan for your life unfolding as you study His Word, pray for wisdom, and practice wise living?
- *Wisdom lives under God's control.* You don't have to live under the "control" of alcohol, sex, power, or the world's other offerings. Wise living comes from being filled and controlled by God's Spirit. Ask Him to be your source of contentment, excitement, and comfort. Let Him guide you every day.

From God's Word to Your Heart

God's ultimate wisdom and plan for you is to "be filled with the Spirit" (Ephesians 5:18). Paul isn't referring to the Holy Spirit's indwelling at salvation here. He is giving a command for believers to live continually under the influence of the Holy Spirit. He is charging you (and me) to walk in wisdom as you live moment-by-moment under the control and guidance of the Holy Spirit. What a difference that will make in your heart, in your conduct, in your priorities, and in the ways you choose to use your time.

Lord, I'm under the influence of the Holy Spirit. I'm practicing Your wisdom and discovering the joys of being obedient and faithful. I no longer lean on the world's offering of what is best or right. I know the truth because it is in Your Word and in my heart. Amen.

Suffering for Doing Good

For what credit is it if, when you are beaten
for your faults, you take it patiently? But when you do good
and suffer, if you take it patiently,
this is commendable before God.

1 Peter 2:20

In Peter's day, slavery was a way of life. Probably quite a few believers in Jesus worked for pagans as slaves or servants. Many in the early church who heard Peter's letter read were slaves—some to masters who were good and considerate, and others to those who were harsh and cruel. This was the situation of the day and the social structure of that time. Being a servant or a slave required having a teachable spirit, being humble, and showing deference.

Peter's instructions let us know we're called to Christlikeness in every situation and in every relationship. This too requires a gentle, teachable spirit. Peter has much to teach us about developing a gentleness that doesn't cause disturbances and a quietness of heart that doesn't respond to the disturbances caused by others.

Although you're not a slave...and most employers aren't your masters, having a job often requires the same attributes...or at least rewards those attributes. What have your work experiences been like? If you hold down a paying job now or if you've had one in the past, have you been blessed with kind employers? Or perhaps you've tasted the cup of cruelty and meanness? Have you endured a distracting or difficult coworker? Our natural tendency is to fight unfair and unreasonable treatment. Peter reminds us that when we suffer for doing good, it is commendable before God. If you're enduring pain for doing good, it's not in vain!

From God's Word to Your Heart

Whether we work for an individual or a company, we need to obey the directives of our employers. But if we're asked to violate God's Word, we have the freedom to say no and change jobs. There is...

...a right way to respond to our bosses and supervisors—to submit

...a right motive for submission—praise from God

...a right attitude toward those "over" us—respect

...a right reason for suffering for doing good—becoming like Jesus

...a right manner for enduring suffering—patiently

These "rights" rule out a lot of wrongs, including rebellion, anger, a bad attitude, hostility, ambition, disdain, discontent, pride, gossip, undermining, shirking, lip service, and revenge. And I'm sure you can add to the list!

> *Lord, I endeavor to do the right thing in my job situation. And I work hard to be successful and please my employer. But most of all I want my work and effort to honor You. Help me see where my attitude is negative, where I need to change. I want to be a servant who submits willingly to You. I pray that my following Your instructions will ultimately lead people to You. Amen.*

Obtaining God's Reward

Those who have served well as deacons obtain
for themselves a good standing and great boldness
in the faith which is in Christ Jesus.

1 Timothy 3:13

Isn't it a wonderful feeling to be proud of someone you love? I've had those special moments. After having faithfully served as a pharmacy officer in the U.S. Army Reserves for more than 20 years, my husband, Jim, retired. In standard military fashion, the entire family was invited to his retirement ceremony. I was in awe of the formal ceremony, the full military band, the two-star general's helicopter that landed on the field, bringing him in to pin on medals and hand out award certificates signed by the president of the United States for those being honored. What a celebration!

This honor was awarded to Jim because of one thing—his faithful service. Even though receiving awards and rewards is never to be a motive for faithfulness, church leaders too can and should receive recognition for their faithful service. As the book of Timothy illuminates, a leader of godly character gains two rewards:

🦅 *Reward 1—A good standing.* This speaks of community respect and a positive, strong reputation.

☞ *Reward 2—Great boldness in faith.* When a leader faithfully discharges his duties and constantly strives to meet the qualifications of a deacon, he or she will have the personal integrity to speak boldly—and brilliantly!—as a representative of Jesus Christ to those who are lost.

Paul says that faithful service will result in the reward of recognition by the church and by the community, by believers and unbelievers. A faithful servant's character provides a platform to share his or her faith boldly. Do you want this reward, this opportunity to lead others to Christ?

From God's Word to Your Heart

Faithfulness is a high calling. You and I want to be faithful so we can please and honor our Lord Jesus. We don't look for recognition, but we will encounter rewards if we do well in our arenas of service. Faithfulness is not one heroic act. Instead, it's an everyday kind of commitment to service. So let's quietly… and faithfully…go about the everyday business of serving others in our roles as wives, mothers, daughters, aunts, mentors, and women of God.

In what areas of your life do you want to aspire to greater service and faithfulness? Do you depend on God's strength as you fulfill the vital responsibilities He's given to you? Your godliness will benefit others and be a beacon of light in a dark world. And it will yield rich rewards for you.

God, I will strive to be faithful and to serve in Your name with honor and integrity. May I be one of Your lights to the world. Amen.

Beginning in Ministry

When [Jesus] was twelve…the boy Jesus lingered behind in
Jerusalem…They found [Jesus] in the temple,
sitting in the midst of the teachers.

LUKE 2:42-43,46

Now Jesus Himself began His ministry
at about thirty years of age.

LUKE 3:23

I've heard it said that "success is when preparation meets
opportunity." Preparation gives you and me the ability to seize
opportunities as they come. That's what happened in my ministry
life. During my private years at home—years of ministry devoted
to raising my children, supporting my busy pastor-husband, and
running a busy home—I studied my Bible and sought growth
in my Christian life. Then one day, when my children were older,
a different kind of opportunity came along. Our church needed
women to teach in a newly formed women's ministry. Because
I had spent those years in preparation, I hesitantly volunteered
my services…and, in God's timing and with His great grace,
my public ministry was born. That teaching ministry eventually
developed into a speaking and writing ministry.

In chapter 3 of Luke, we discover that John the Baptist and

Jesus spent close to 30 years preparing for the days when they would begin their ministries. During this time, they were actively living in God's will. Their preparation was fulfilling prophecy and God's plan for mankind's salvation. From their example we learn that if we desire to minister to others, we need to start with preparation...and then wait for God to provide the opportunities.

From God's Word to Your Heart

Even the most patient of us rarely likes to wait very long. But when we consider that our time of waiting is also a time of preparation, that changes our outlook.

When John the Baptist baptized Jesus, it was God's perfect timing for Jesus' preparation to be turned into ministry action. As we know, Jesus didn't wait or hold back until age 30 to bless and to serve others, but that's when His official ministry started.

Unfortunately, many Christians fail to ever begin preparing to minister to the body of Christ. To live with passion and purpose means we are aggressively taking advantage of each day to help others *and* gear up for greater things. We're spending time in preparation so we will be ready when more opportunities to serve the Lord come our way.

Are you preparing for ministry today? Are you actively helping others? What can you do to continue preparing for more service to the Lord and those around you?

> *Lord, I pray to be walking in Your will each day. I want to always be actively involved in Your ministry. Help me discover ways I can prepare so I can be of more service to You and Your people. Guide me, lead me...and I will gladly follow. Amen.*

Breaking Down Barriers

[Jesus] is our peace, who has made both one, and has
broken down the middle wall of separation.

EPHESIANS 2:14

Peace is something we not only want but need. We seek peace, march for peace, pray for peace, even go to war for peace. However, Jesus Christ is the only way to true peace and the only source of true peace for every person. And Christ is also the way and the source of peace among all believers in the body of Christ. Each Christian comes from a different background, upbringing, lineage, and environment. In Christ we are unified.

Before the coming of Jesus, Jews and Gentiles shunned each other. However, in grace, Christ offered His salvation to both. Yet barriers still existed between the two groups. For instance, in the Jewish temple there was a wall that separated the Jews from the Gentiles as they worshipped. Spiritually Christ abolished that physical wall in the temple and in all areas of worship.

Only Christ could, can, and does break down every wall of division. And only Christ could, can, and does reconcile believers to God and unify them in one body. Ask Christ to remove all the barriers that negatively affect your view, opinion, and respect of other Christians, regardless of race, wealth, social standing, family ties, and so forth. Consider which situations are robbing you of God's peace and unity with other believers. Give those situations to God in prayer. Make Christ's peace the foundation for all your thinking, your speech, and your actions towards others.

From God's Word to Your Heart

Jim and I have some incredible neighbors—a husband and wife who both serve their country through military service. In recent years one was deployed to Iraq and the other to Afghanistan, with the goal of bringing peace to those countries. When their tours of duty were complete, instead of coming home, their units remained deployed because the goal of peace hadn't yet been achieved. Peace is still not a reality.

History reveals that most human peace missions fail. But the peace achieved by the blood of Christ is real and eternal. I hope you've grasped the peace our Savior accomplished between you and God, and between you and all believers.

What wells up in your heart and soul as you recall the moment when the barrier between you and God was removed? As Paul noted, you were once far off from the Father, but have now been brought near to Him. And the same is true of all those in the body of Christ. My friend, we are all in the Father's embrace.

Lord, You removed the barriers that divided me from You and from others who believe in You. Thank You for giving me a clear path to peace through You. You are my light. Amen.

Conquering by Continuing

I do not count myself to have apprehended; but one thing I do, forgetting those things which are behind and reaching forward to those things which are ahead, I press toward the goal for the prize of the upward call of God in Christ Jesus.

PHILIPPIANS 3:13-14

One of my favorite verses is 2 Corinthians 5:17: "If anyone is in Christ, he is a new creation; old things have passed away; behold, all things have become new." It's so comforting to know that in salvation my past sins and failures are wiped away by God's grace. How thrilling to know that as Christians we are new creatures in Christ! But this doesn't mean we've reached spiritual perfection. We must press on, like runners in a race—a race of life and faith. We need to concentrate our energies on moving forward. What does a runner need?

- *Mental obliteration.* Runners never look back. They forget the part of the course already covered and focus forward.
- *Unwavering progression.* Runners strain every nerve and muscle to keep moving with all their might toward the goal. They are thinking, *I want this win!*
- *A goal in view.* Runners' eyes are always fixed on the finish line.

If your heart and feet try to move forward but your mind and eyes are turned toward the past, you aren't going to reach your destination anytime soon. Is anything hindering your forward focus? "Lay aside every weight, and the sin which so easily ensnares [you], and…run with endurance the race that is set before [you]" (Hebrews 12:1).

From God's Word to Your Heart

"But one thing I do…" How would you finish this statement? The famous preacher D.L. Moody wrote these words from a scholar named Gannett in the margin of his Bible beside Philippians 3:13: "Men may be divided into two classes—those who have a 'one thing' and those who have no 'one thing' to do; those with aim, and those without aim in their lives…The aim in life is what the backbone is to the body: Without it we are invertebrate."

How frightening it would be to be "invertebrate"—to be spineless, weak, and weak willed—especially in the Christian life. But thanks be to God for these cherished-yet-instructive verses about the process whereby you and I can know and accomplish our "one thing"—attaining the great prize of the Christian race.

Are you refusing to look back? Are you pressing and straining forward with unwavering faith? Are you looking to the prize of the upward call of God in Christ Jesus? May you faithfully continue on and finish the race well!

Lord, I press on in hot pursuit of the call You've made on my life. I won't turn to stare at my past stumbles and fumbles. Instead I'll continue to look forward toward spiritual growth, a deeper dependence on You, and the prize of purpose in You. Amen.

Living in Peace

Greet one another with a kiss of love.
Peace to you all who are in Christ Jesus. Amen.

1 PETER 5:14

As a writer, I know that endings are difficult. I always hope to leave you with some kind of positive sensation—about your life, about your future, about God's message, and about Him—yet also motivate you to move out on the truths you've just learned. Peter faced this same dilemma as he was forced to lay down his pen.

It's probable that Peter hadn't even met the people who would read his letter...and that he would never meet them. But knowing of their struggles and being a shepherd at heart, Peter wrote. And his subject matter—suffering for doing what is right—was certainly something he knew all too well. He'd witnessed the suffering of his friend and Savior. He knew all about the hounding crowds, the belligerent rulers, the ranks of armed soldiers, the brutal trials, the cross.

After writing a letter that was so much about suffering and perseverance, his ending word selection was very intentional. Read the verse for today again. They are words of unity, love, and peace written carefully many years ago—and yet so powerful for our faith journey today.

I've learned there are two kinds of peace needed in the arena of life, both available to us from and through God: *personal peace* and *interpersonal peace.* Everyone's been in situations where there's strife and malice with others. And it can be so easy to succumb to our negative emotions and actively engage in the conflict. Thank God for making His peace—*our ability to promote interpersonal peace*—available through His Holy Spirit! God will help us honor Him in our responses: "A soft answer turns away wrath, but a harsh word stirs up anger" (Proverbs 15:1).

And then there is the area of *personal peace,* which is sorely needed when facing terror, fear, panic, dread, doubt, and restlessness of spirit. For these deeply felt difficulties and sorrows, Peter includes this powerful word of reminder: *Peace.* How can you seek and secure God's peace in your daily life?

- Take your tendency to *panic*…and instead rest in God's *presence.*
- Take your tendency to *terror*…and instead *trust* in God's wisdom and ways.
- Take your tendency to *dread*…and instead accept God's *dealings.*
- Take your tendency to *nervousness*…and instead *know* God is in control.

Peter was with the Lord when He said, "Peace I leave with you, My peace I give to you; not as the world gives do I give to you. Let not your heart be troubled, neither let it be afraid" (John 14:27). And now Peter passes on to us the very essence of the personal words Jesus spoke to Peter and the other disciples as they faced what was to come: "Peace to you all who are in Christ Jesus. Amen."

Lord, thank You for Your peace. During times of turmoil with others or trials that are heavy on my heart, Your peace is sufficient and ever-present. May I seek You with the cup of my heart and be filled again and again with the sweet, calming peace of You. Amen.

Caring for Widows

Honor widows who are really widows. But if any widow
has children or grandchildren, let them first learn to show
piety at home and to repay their parents; for this is good
and acceptable before God...If anyone does not provide for
his own, and especially for those of his household, he has
denied the faith and is worse than an unbeliever.

1 TIMOTHY 5:3-4,8

The thought of becoming a widow isn't pleasant. But according
to life insurance statistics, most married women will outlive their
husbands. Not only do widows face the emotional loss of their
partners, but many of them also face the burden of significant
financial loss. Widows in AD 63, when Timothy was pastoring,
didn't have the safety nets of today, such as insurance or retirement plans. They were completely at the mercy of others. Many
were looking to the church for help, and the church was having
difficulty carrying the burden. So Paul makes a point to say who
should take care of the widows. This is a message for all of us.

Family members are to provide for the widows within the
family. While we, as the church, are also supposed to care for
those in need, Paul tells it like it is: "If anyone does not provide
for his own, and especially for those of his household, he has
denied the faith and is worse than an unbeliever" (1 Timothy

5:8). That's a strong statement, but it's so true! Are we ready to care for our mothers and mothers-in-law when the time comes? Are we raising children who will respect us and the Word of God to help care for us one day?

Well, it's heart-to-heart time. And this is truly from my heart to yours. I remember telling a group of women that my husband, Jim, and I don't pray about taking care of our parents. That's because it is a "given." The Scripture says to care for them, so that's what we planned to do. We'd just do it. Well, I have to tell you that *I* was shocked when I noticed the shock on *their* faces. And we had quite a discussion. But there it is, right in 1 Timothy 5. This verse moved us to make the decision regarding our families long ago. And after caring for all of our parents through their declining years, we have no regrets. It wasn't easy by any means, but there were many moments of joy along the way.

One thing that a woman who loves God does is care for her family members. Yes, it takes time, money, and effort. But it's also good and acceptable in the sight of *God*.

> *Lord, give me eyes to see the needs present in my own family. Give me a loving heart and the courage to act on meeting their needs. God, You promised to care for the widow, the orphan, and those who call on Your name. May I serve You by serving them faithfully. Amen.*

Putting On the Armor of God

Stand therefore, having girded your waist with truth,
having put on the breastplate of righteousness, and having
shod your feet with the preparation of the gospel of peace;
above all, taking the shield of faith with which you will be
able to quench all the fiery darts of the wicked one. And
take the helmet of salvation, and the sword of the Spirit,
which is the word of God; praying always…

EPHESIANS 6:14-18

As an author, what's happening around me often shows up in
my books. The same thing occurs in Paul's writing as he explains
the reality of spiritual warfare. Paul pens this letter from a prison
where, for two years, he's been observing Roman soldiers daily.
Because he learned a lot about the soldiers' armor and weaponry,
he uses it to remind us to prepare for spiritual battle.

From God's Word to Your Heart

Have you struggled to rest in the Bible's truth? To stand for
God? To follow Christ faithfully? Take heart! You're not alone.
These battles are part of a great spiritual war involving this world…
and the entire universe. Praise God, the ultimate victory has been

won by Christ! What can you do to ensure you are strong and will be victorious in your stand against Satan?

Put on truth. Soldiers wore a belt around their waists to hold pieces of armor in place. The belt of truth is essential for doing battle against the lies, half-truths, and distortions of Satan.

Put on the breastplate of righteousness. The breastplate provided a soldier with protection from the neck to the thighs. Righteousness is holiness, and your faithful obedience to Christ forms a protective covering.

Put on the gospel of peace. A Roman soldier had special sandals made of soft leather with studded soles that allowed him to stand firm in combat. Putting on truth enables you to stand your ground against Satan's lies.

Pick up the shield of faith. The large Roman shield was designed for full protection. Faith is your shield. Trusting and believing God is involved in everything you hold to and have confidence in.

Put on the helmet of salvation. The helmet protected a soldier's head from arrows and sword blows. "Salvation" is referring to your future eternal life and heaven. The helmet of salvation gives you confidence that a great and glorious victory is coming.

Wield the sword of the Spirit. The sword spoken of here was used in hand-to-hand combat. This spiritual weapon has its origin in the Spirit of God, who teaches you what the Bible means and how to apply it in your daily life.

Dressing for spiritual success is a head-to-toe process. Putting on and wearing this armor, you can win the daily struggles of living for Christ wholeheartedly.

> *Lord, I will follow You into spiritual battle dressed for victory. May I never take for granted my faith. Remind me to use it as my shield each day. Guide me with Your strength. Each victory is to Your glory. Amen.*

Living in Faith

Count it all joy when you fall into various trials, knowing
that the testing of your faith produces patience. But let
patience have its perfect work, that you may be perfect
and complete, lacking nothing.

JAMES 1:2-4

Have you had teachers who were blunt when presenting instruction and very upfront about your challenges? These are often the best mentors we'll encounter. James is one such teacher. He's practical and to the point as he addresses internal problems that hurt us and can undermine our Christian lives. When you look at the following list, you'll more than likely recognize yourself and some of the challenges you deal with.

- ☞ spiritual distress
- ☞ wrong living caused by wrong doctrine
- ☞ a general, low spiritual state
- ☞ wrong attitudes toward the goodness of God and His gifts

These lead to

- ☞ indulgence in unbridled speech
- ☞ strife and the creation of factions

☞ the adoption of a worldly spirit

I told you James was practical! And he isn't all about listing problems. He also challenges us to embrace solutions so we can live the Christian life, not just profess it. Are you committed to living up to your faith? To living in a godly manner?

From God's Word to Your Heart

You've faced trials before, and you will face more. Is it really possible to count your troubles as joy like James tells you to? Yes, but it takes spiritual discipline. Here are two ways you can ensure that your faith grows in…and in spite of…trials.

By the use of your mind. Counting trials as joy has to do with your mind and not your emotions. No matter how you feel emotionally or physically, choose to count the situation joy! Know you'll eventually reap blessings of joy, patience, and completion as you look forward to the outcome of your trials—greater spiritual maturity and stronger faith.

By the use of your faith. You can choose to look at each trial with an eye of faith. Why? Because the eye of faith will see the hand of God in every situation. Only faith can track God's kind of bookkeeping that places each trial in the joy column. When you suffer, choose to *believe* in the goodness of God and in His perfecting process of you and your faith. *Believe* during the painful times that God loves you and is in perfect control of all things. *Believe* in the greater-yet-still-veiled purposes of God. And *believe* in the positive results of your testings—a closer relationship with your heavenly Father.

Friend, be encouraged and forge through your troubles. "We do not look at the things which are seen, but at the things which are not seen. For the things which are seen are temporary, but the things which are not seen are eternal" (2 Corinthians 4:18). Now *that's* the way the eye of faith looks at trials!

> *Lord, help me live in faith and believe in Your plan and love and purpose during my trials. I choose to walk forward in this situation with a prayerful heart and an eye of faith. Amen.*

Serving the Lord

[Jesus] entered a certain village; and a certain woman named
Martha welcomed Him into her house. And she had a sister called
Mary, who also sat at Jesus' feet and heard His word. But Martha
was distracted with much serving, and she approached Him and
said, "Lord, do You not care that my sister has left me to serve
alone? Therefore tell her to help me."

LUKE 10:38-40

Martha and Mary. Why do we love these two sisters so much?
Because at times we identify with both of them! Many of us are
women on missions, whether planning a dinner party, home-
schooling our children, making carpool rounds, managing a
household, organizing a ministry, or running a business. With
such pressured and purposed service, it's easy to lose sight of our
need for passionate worship. Yes, purpose and momentum are
needed. We must be Marthas at times. But like Mary, we also
need to pause during our hectic schedules and commune with
the Lord.

Do you more commonly relate to Martha's request for help?
She sees her sister thoroughly enjoying the visit from Jesus while
she feels compelled to make everything perfect for the gathering.
Have you ever hosted a dinner and realized later that you barely
took time to enjoy your guests? I think many of us have Martha
tendencies, so let's embrace what Jesus offers Martha.

Acknowledgment. Jesus expresses empathy. He immediately recognizes the pressure Martha is under when He says, "You are worried and troubled about many things" (Luke 10:41). When we are weary, Jesus sees our trials and our burdens. He knows we are frazzled or frustrated.

Truth. As compassionate as Jesus is, He also leads Martha to the truth. We are to focus on only one thing, and Mary has chosen that one thing—to focus on Jesus and serve and learn from Him (verse 42).

There is nothing more important than sitting at the feet of our Lord!

From God's Word to Your Heart

The Martha vs. Mary pull in us might always take place, but hopefully we'll learn to place our emphasis on "the one thing"... the right Person...Jesus. When we take time to worship, we discover that communion with God is the starting place of all our service for God and others.

Martha and Mary were so fortunate because they were able to be with Jesus while He was living in bodily form on this earth. They could reach out and touch Him and provide Him with a good meal. And they could sit in His physical presence, talking, asking questions, and laughing.

Although we don't get that, we have Jesus living within us, a constant presence in our lives! What can we do? We can reach out in Jesus' name to someone in need of compassion. We can serve a meal to someone who needs hospitality. We can have ongoing dialogue with God through prayer. We are so blessed! We are in the presence of our Sustainer, and we can take the strength and compassion we draw from Him to serve Him by sharing it with those in our world.

> *Lord, I want to sit at Your feet as Your disciple and friend. I want to see You smile as I give You praise and share my day. Help me turn my heart to the one thing that matters more than all else...my time with You. Amen.*

Living Above Reproach

But refuse the younger widows; for when they have begun
to grow wanton against Christ, they desire to marry, having
condemnation because they have cast off their first faith.

1 TIMOTHY 5:11-12

The story of *Beauty and the Beast* has been around for a long
time. After reading Paul's words in today's verse, it's clear that
the dynamics of that story have been around a lot longer. We first
meet *beauty* in the form of the older, faithful widow:

Do not let a widow under sixty years old be taken into
the number, and not unless she has been the wife of one
man, well reported for good works: if she has brought up
children, if she has lodged strangers, if she has washed
the saints' feet, if she has relieved the afflicted, if she has
diligently followed every good work (1 Timothy 5:9-10).

Now, brace yourself for the *beast*. Paul turns his (and our)
attention to the younger widows and points out their character
flaws and sinful choices:

[The younger widows] have begun to grow wanton against
Christ, they desire to marry, having condemnation because
they have cast off their first faith. And besides they learn
to be idle, wandering about from house to house, and not

only idle but also gossips and busybodies, saying things which they ought not (verses 11-13).

What are the younger widows focused on?

> *Sensual desire*—Tempted by sexual pleasures, these young women ignored their virtue and their faith by pursuing adulterous relationships with men.

> *Idleness*—The young widows aren't working or tending to children, so they are filling their time with frivolous, useless activity and gossip.

> *Separated from faith*—Without righteous husbands to lead them, many young widows lost interest in their original faith. They often married men of other religions and adopted their pagan ways.

These beastly attitudes can happen in any woman who steps away from godly instruction and decides that her personal desires are more important than those of the Lord.

From God's Word to Your Heart

There is such a difference between the beauty of the "good works" of the older widows and the scandalous, destructive "works" of the on-the-go younger group. What wasted time…and energy… and lives! What missed opportunities to do something useful, to better the lives of others, to do something constructive and of eternal value.

I want to leave you with three qualities I encourage you to develop that will help you, whether you're married, single, widowed, young, or old.

> *Self-control.* Any woman can give in to sensuality and

dishonor the name of Christ. Keep these behaviors in check and remain pure as women of God.

- ⚜ *Servant behavior.* Bad habits are most often produced by idleness. If we take precious time away from our families and our service to God by watching too much television, talking on the phone, and skimming the Internet, we'll become busybodies instead of busy servants.

- ⚜ *Faithful.* A commitment to marriage and family fills our hearts and creates in us an even greater desire to honor Christ and serve those in our homes and our communities.

Lord, when I'm tempted to fill my time with worldly pleasures and useless activities, help me follow the ways of the older widows. They remained faithful and righteous. Like them I desire to live above reproach. I want to be beautiful in and for You. Amen.

Counting on God's Peace

Paul and Timothy, bondservants of Jesus Christ,
to all the saints in Christ Jesus who are in Philippi, with the
bishops and deacons: Grace to you and peace from God our
Father and the Lord Jesus Christ.

PHILIPPIANS 1:1-2

Have you been separated from someone you dearly love and long to communicate with? That's the reason Paul took pen in hand and wrote a letter to the Philippians. He had a lot to say. He wanted to express his love for the people of Philippi and thank them. He also wanted to comfort them, but he also needed to warn and correct them about a few things. This is one incredible correspondence!

But did you notice something even more remarkable in today's Scripture verses? That a great leader like the apostle Paul and his right-hand man, Timothy, chose to evaluate and describe themselves as "bondservants" of Jesus Christ.

The Greek word Paul used for "servant" was *doulos,* which refers to a slave who had no rights, no possessions, no authority even over his or her own person. Instead, he was the possession of another...forever. A slave's role in life was singular: To obey his or her master's will quickly, quietly, and without question.

How often have we signed letters as *doulos* of Christ? (I know

I never have.) What changes in attitude would need to be made so that we could proclaim with Paul and Timothy that we're bondservants to Christ—and mean it with all our hearts?

We are so fortunate to be God's women! The twin resources of God's grace and God's peace are ours:

- *God's grace* is His unmerited favor poured out upon those who have trusted in Jesus Christ. The sustaining power of God is packaged within His grace and favor! Just as God is all we need, so God's grace covers everything we can think of and more.

- *God's peace* is ours when we approach Him with child-like confidence and trust and hope, knowing He is our heavenly Father who watches over us and takes care of us in every way. Truly we have peace with God, the peace of God, and the God of peace—all we need for total well-being.

What is your most pressing trial or difficulty today? Tap into those two supernatural resources—God's power and God's peace. They're available and all yours if you belong to the family of God through Jesus Christ. Isn't that awe inspiring?

The challenges of truly being a servant, a saint, and a possessor of God's supernatural resources of grace and peace are ones we can face together. Strive to be a servant of the Lord Most High, a woman who has no other master but Him. Be completely sold out to Jesus! When the challenge seems too great, look to the Lord and count on His grace and power. He'll see you through!

Lord, I want to be Your slave. With the power and might of Your grace and peace, help me live a life that pleases You. Remind me that You are the perfect Master. Give me the heart of a faithful servant. Amen.

Praying Always

Pray in the Spirit on all occasions with all kinds of prayers
and requests. With this in mind, be alert and always keep
on praying for all the saints. Pray also for me, that whenever
I open my mouth, words may be given me so that I will
fearlessly make known the mystery of the gospel, for which I
am an ambassador in chains.

EPHESIANS 6:18-19 NIV

My husband was in the Army Reserves for more than 20 years. Jim was never in combat, but every time he went off for training or was called up, the potential was there and the chances for harm increased. And because I didn't always know where he was or what he was doing, the only thing I could do was pray for God's protection to surround him.

Have there been times when you were so removed from the action or the event of concern that you felt helpless? Or maybe you question whether your gifts and abilities can be used by God. Sometimes young stay-at-home moms feel like they're on the sidelines when it comes to Christian ministry. And women can get so caught up in the stress of the work-for-pay world they lose sight of what they can do for the Lord…if they even have the energy to contemplate it. Then there are those homebound women who suffer ill health. There are so many different situations that might pull you down so you feel ineffective. The good news is that you—as a believer—can participate in the most important course of action possible. What is that? Prayer!

Through prayer God allows you to be part of the frontline of spiritual battles, a participant in global ministries, and a source of wisdom, encouragement, and help to your family.

From God's Word to Your Heart

I wish I could talk with you personally and get to know you. Even though I can't do that, I'm sure you face many of the challenges I face—personal problems, worries, anxieties, temptations, disappointments, and more. The problems that challenge you are very real and your concerns are legitimate. Studies have shown that when a greater anxiety or concern comes along, the lesser ones fade away.

What does that mean? If you want to be free of your worries and anxieties, then lose yourself in the real issues of life—the relationships that really matter, the issues close to your heart, the spiritual battles you and others face, the second coming of Jesus, and the impact of whether people have chosen God through Jesus or not.

And then what can you do? Pray! Pray always. Pray for those close to you. Pray for those you don't know. Pray for the situations people face. You'll soon discover that it's almost impossible…if not impossible…to worry about yourself and pray for others at the same time. And don't forget to pray for yourself. You want to be strong in the power of God's might and reach out to others with the good news of the gospel.

God, when I pray in the Spirit, I am taking action. You have blessed me with gifts, abilities, and a heart of compassion. Help me see the needs around me and understand what I can do to reach out and help. Teach me to be sensitive to the spiritual battles happening in my area and in the world at large. Remind me to pray faithfully. Thank You for letting me participate in bringing others to You. Amen.

Building God's House

Coming to Him as to a living stone, rejected indeed by
men, but chosen by God and precious, you also,
as living stones, are being built up a spiritual house,
a holy priesthood, to offer up spiritual sacrifices
acceptable to God through Jesus Christ.

1 Peter 2:4-5

Have you had to do something by yourself...utterly alone? Have you been the only one bearing the full weight of a task or an endeavor? And have you ever wished for someone—anyone—to come alongside and give a helping hand, to assist you in carrying just part of the responsibility? You might feel alone in your emotional burdens. Many of us juggle incredible responsibilities in our households, churches, families, and communities, feeling alone in the middle of such busyness and worthwhile efforts.

Wouldn't you agree that it's hard to work alone and to stand alone? Being part of a group certainly has tremendous benefits. And that's the way it is in the body of Christ too. No one is ever alone. We will never be asked to stand alone or minister alone. Why? Because we are a "spiritual house" that is constructed using many individual "living stones." God provided for us so we'd never be alone.

I thank God for Peter, the verbal artist who has used superb imagery to paint a picture of the body of Christ that is simultaneously comforting and challenging. In 1 Peter 2:6, he tells us, "Behold, I lay in Zion a chief cornerstone, elect, precious, and he who believes on Him will by no means be put to shame," which is based on Isaiah 28:16. We are building our eternal life on the chief cornerstone (Jesus), and we are supported by other living stones when we reach out in fellowship with other believers. Isn't that comforting?

There's nothing we, as believers, will have to do alone or bear alone. Why? Because we're part of a "spiritual house"—the church of God. And what is this house like? Its foundation is Christ. As a house, it possesses strength and beauty based on a wide variety of materials (including you!). What's more, this magnificent house of God is built up and improved with the addition of each person when they accept Christ and become new members of His family.

And how is the picture of the church, the body of Christ, challenging? It requires that you and I, as individuals, do our part to sustain the strength, beauty, and usefulness of the house. We have to let go of our impulses to do our own thing, on our own strength, in our own timing. We need to focus on the Lord and ask Him what He wants us to do...and when...and where...and how. And He will tell us! Rest in this freedom today.

God, I have felt alone. I have tried to live my life without support, without leaning on You as my cornerstone. In my hurry to live a good life, I've sometimes forgotten that I'm not meant to live it alone. Thank You for reminding me I live with You in Your magnificent house. Amen.

Discovering the Secret to Wisdom

If any of you lacks wisdom, let him ask of God,
who gives to all liberally and without reproach,
and it will be given to him.

JAMES 1:5

Do you want in on a really good secret? I heard it from James, and he said I could share it with you. He said, in essence, "Let me tell you a secret that will revolutionize your life as you encounter the various trials life sends your way. A secret that will bring about greater endurance, character, wisdom, and faith in you!" Doesn't that sound exciting?

As we dream about possessing these desirable qualities, James tells us the secret: If you want wisdom, all you have to do is ask God for it. Do you want wisdom for handling your problems? Then go to the only source of truth—to the giving God who bestows wisdom for managing life's trials—and ask.

Are you growing as a woman of faith? As a woman who asks God wholeheartedly, trusts Him completely, and doubts nothing? Are you completely convinced that God's way is always best? Or do you sometimes treat God's Word like it's advice you can take or leave? Do you grapple with what to choose based on your feelings, the world's advice, and God's commands? Do you believe God cares about you? That He is powerful and good and watching over you?

These are serious questions, and the answers will reveal where you are in your walk with God. Do you need to pray about making some changes?

How many times a day do you need God's wisdom? As I write these words, it's almost noon, and I've already counted on God's wisdom several times today. Isn't it wonderful that all you have to do is ask Him for guidance with a heart full of faith...and wisdom will be given to you? The next time you face your trials or dilemmas, instead of praying for the removal of your test, ask God to give you the wisdom needed to handle it His way. Stop, look, and listen before you move ahead full speed:

Stop before you do anything. This gives you time to consult the Lord before you act.

Look to the Lord. Boldly ask, "Lord, what do You want me to do here?"

Listen for His wisdom. A heart of faith believes God hears your cry for help...and He answers.

Proceed because you know God's wisdom is best. Respond to Him in obedience without doubt.

These actions and attitudes of faith make up the secret to wisdom. You will face trial after trial, but you now know *how* to face them!

Lord, I will stop, look, listen, and then proceed. I'm asking today for Your guidance. Help me to discover the secret to wisdom, to discern Your Word and Your will so I can move forward as a woman growing in You. Amen.

Getting Right with God

Beware of the leaven of the Pharisees, which is hypocrisy.
For there is nothing covered that will not be revealed,
nor hidden that will not be known. Therefore whatever you
have spoken in the dark will be heard in the light,
and what you have spoken in the ear in inner rooms will be
proclaimed on the housetops.

LUKE 12:1-3

In ancient times dishonest potters sometimes poured wax into the imperfections of a clay pot and then painted over the flaws, producing what appeared to be a perfect vessel. Only as a pot was lifted to the light could its true nature be determined by a prospective buyer.

We can be thankful that Jesus is straightforward in His teaching on the standards God sets for those who would be kingdom citizens. Dishonesty in all its forms, including hypocrisy, was at the top of Jesus' list of vile sins. If we take time with today's Scripture selection, we see that there are warnings to heed:

- Everything we try to cover up will be uncovered.
- Anything hidden will be revealed.
- Words spoken in the darkness will come to light.
- Comments made to someone in private will be proclaimed.

There is no place for hypocrisy in a life that is faithful and devoted to Christ. Anything said or done in secret—from sharing gossip or acting on sinful impulses—will be revealed. When we hold our lives and conduct up to the light of God's Word, are they pleasing to God?

From God's Word to Your Heart

As we think about living with passion and purpose, we see once again that Jesus remained passionate about His message, especially as He moved toward the cross. Sadly, His sermon on hypocrisy further inflamed the fear and subsequent hatred of the religious leaders toward Him. Yet His message is loud and clear: All must get right with God. Judgment is coming. By immersing ourselves in God's passionate instruction and love, you and I are striving to become a pot without flaws. A pot made whole and perfect through salvation and grace.

Are you facing opposition to your faith at home? At work? From extended family members? Jesus warned that division would come. Ask God to help you stand firm in Him. And what about the coming judgment? Ask God to give you the love and boldness to speak of Jesus' return, even to those who are hostile. Don't give up on others. Jesus didn't.

> *God, grant me discernment and a convicted heart so that I will come clean and unveil all my sins to You. I want to be made perfect in You so my faith will be seen by others and they'll want to know You. Help me live a life that will hold up under scrutiny as one who has received Your grace and healing and serves You wholeheartedly. Amen.*

Giving Thanks for God's Mercy

And I thank Christ Jesus our Lord who has enabled
me, because He counted me faithful, putting me into
the ministry, although I was formerly a blasphemer, a
persecutor, and an insolent man; but I obtained mercy
because I did it ignorantly in unbelief.

1 TIMOTHY 1:12-13

Don't you love weddings? A wedding is a wonderful celebration
of the union between husband and wife and the start of a new
journey together. What a great time to reflect on the power of love!
Another event that leads me to celebrate love and the beginning
of a new journey is Sunday night at our church. Why? Because
that's when our church baptizes new believers. How blessed we
are to hear the wonderful testimonies of those who have been
delivered from darkness. It's so inspiring to bask in the divine
experiences of saved sinners giving thanks to God for His mercy
and looking forward to eternity with Him.

Did you read today's verse? Why not read it again? It's like a
comet streaking across a black sky at night! Paul's testimony of
his salvation shows us the "glorious gospel of the blessed God"!
We get to see Paul's new journey in Christ compared to his old
journey without the Messiah in his life. What a difference! I hope
you've made the decision to follow Christ too.

As saved sinners, you can give thanks to God by celebrating and honoring your...

- *salvation.* Paul never "got over" his salvation...and neither should you! As you reflect back upon your own experience, what words from 1 Timothy 1:13-16 describe God's work in your life?

  > Although I was formerly a blasphemer, a persecutor, and an insolent man; but I obtained mercy because I did it ignorantly in unbelief. And the grace of our Lord was exceedingly abundant, with faith and love which are in Christ Jesus. This is a faithful saying and worthy of all acceptance, that Christ Jesus came into the world to save sinners, of whom I am chief.

- *strength.* Paul thanked Jesus Christ for enabling him to be in the ministry (verse 12).

- *service.* Christ not only saves us, but He strengthens and trains us for service, to share the gospel message with others.

From God's Word to Your Heart

Wow! My heart is overflowing with gratitude to God and Christ Jesus. As Paul put it, "And the grace of our Lord was exceedingly abundant, with faith and love which are in Christ Jesus" (1 Timothy 1:14). Paul is telling us that God's grace is "super abundant" and way more than adequate for all our sins.

Why not do as Paul did? Why not make his response your response? Give thanks to God for His mercy. Burst forth in a doxology—praising, giving praise, and expressing glory to God. Spend time now in an outpouring of praise and glory to God.

(You may also want to write it out. And why not share it with others?)

Lord, thank You for Your sweet mercy. It has covered my sinful past and provided me with a new journey that ends in eternity with You. May my life be an example of Your saving grace and my deep gratitude. Amen.

Benefiting Through Trials

Blessed is the man who endures temptation; for when he
has been proved, he will receive the crown of life which the
Lord has promised to those who love Him.

JAMES 1:12

Each trial that comes our way is like a body of water that
must be crossed. And there's only one way to cross a body of
water, my friend, and that's to get into a boat, push away from
the comfort of the shore (from our present spiritual state), and
set sail. To successfully navigate each new trial we must set sail,
and we must stay in the boat until it reaches the other side. There
are no shortcuts.

Whether you're facing a significant temptation, a huge obstacle, or a painful loss, your journey of endurance requires that
you don't jump ship. You can't bail out. You can't panic. You
can't waver in your commitment to ride it out. No, you stay
in the boat.

Each new test calls for you to use the wisdom and maturity
you possess. And it challenges you to once again trust the Lord
and call on Him for strength and wisdom. The really good
news is that when you reach the other side of the trial, you've
grown spiritually! Wonderful, noticeable, real spiritual growth
has taken place.

God's truth is universal. No matter where you start, no matter the condition of the port you're leaving, you can apply God's message to your personal situation with absolute faith. God will ease your burdens if you just ask.

The lowly. If you live on meager means, you're called upon by James to rejoice and to glory in the fact that, as a Christian, you're a child of God and a joint heir with Christ (Romans 8:16-17). Even if you're not wealthy you can glory and rejoice in the Lord.

The rich. If you've been blessed with wealth and material goods, James essentially says, "Be sure you put no store in your riches. Life is uncertain. As quickly as the newly risen sun wilts and withers the grass, so your riches can disappear. Don't place your trust in external things you can lose in a second. Trust instead in the Lord and in the eternal riches only He can provide."

You will experience suffering. And in the end you know one thing for sure: The ground at the foot of the cross is level. Trials are the great equalizer, leveling all believers to dependence on God. So persevere, knowing you will receive the blessing of the crown of life that the Lord has promised to those who love Him.

> *Lord, it's scary to leave the port I know so well...even when it's become a place of suffering. In this trial I'm facing, I'm going to set sail, depending on Your promises to navigate, keep me safe, and provide the wisdom I need to reach the other side. Amen.*

Counting On God's Inheritance

In Him also we have obtained an inheritance,
being predestined according to the purpose of Him who
works all things according to the counsel of His will,
that we who first trusted in Christ should be to
the praise of His glory.

EPHESIANS 1:11-12

My parents were both schoolteachers who worked hard all their lives. After years of teaching, they both retired and followed a mutual passion of buying, restoring, and selling antiques. They managed to accumulate enough funds to provide a small inheritance for me and my three brothers. Jim and I used my share to pay down our home mortgage. Every day as I walk through my home I think of my dear, sweet parents and their gift to me and my family.

Maybe you won't have an inheritance from an earthly father—but take heart! Your heavenly Father has given you a heavenly inheritance that you can count on. As you walk through your life with a sense of security, think of your Father's gift to you and what that means.

Your life in Christ. When you trust in God's Word and believe in His inheritance, you will feel compelled to respond with gratitude. Your words, actions, and heart are transformed as you live in Christ.

Your attachment to the world. What a relief to know that your real wealth and value is in your identity in Christ and your salvation. You don't need the world's version of riches. Your blessings as a child of God are your greatest treasures.

Your mission to others. You heard the good news and responded. Now it's your turn to reach out to others. Do something today that shares the gospel of Christ with others. Give from your heavenly inheritance by showing others what it means to receive the gifts of God's love and grace.

From God's Word to Your Heart

As a believer in Jesus Christ and one who trusts in Him, you've been given an inheritance in Him that is sealed and guaranteed by the Holy Spirit. But you weren't saved and blessed for your own glory. No, it was for *God's* glory. Your redemption becomes an example of God's great grace for others. When they see how God moves in your life, they will want to know God and be led by Him. Isn't it incredible that God allows you to assist Him in such a personal and lasting way?

Paul formed an exceptional habit of praise that is a great model for you. In Ephesians 1:6 he praised God. In verse 12 he praised Jesus Christ. And he informs us that the Holy Spirit's work will be to the praise of God's glory. Give God your heart response of praise. Make it your habit to praise Him. It's one thing you do on earth that you will continue to do in heaven.

Lord, I'm so grateful to receive Your heavenly inheritance. I walk through my days with a heart full of praise and thanksgiving. May my life reflect how grateful I am for the blessings You've given to me...and continue to give me. Thank You! I praise You for my hope, my future, and my faith in You. Amen.

Living with Heaven in View

For to me, to live is Christ, and to die is gain.
But if I live on in the flesh, this will mean fruit from my labor;
yet what I shall choose I cannot tell. For I am
hard-pressed between the two, having a desire to depart
and be with Christ, which is far better.

PHILIPPIANS 1:21-23

Dying isn't a very popular...or comfortable...subject for most of us. One child wrote, "Dear God, what is it like when you die? Nobody will tell me. I just want to know. I don't want to do it!" Adults don't ask that in case we find out the "hard" way. No, we'd rather read about the how-to's of living the good life.

When English Puritan Richard Baxter lay dying at age 76, racked with pain and disease, a friend asked him, "How are you?" His reply? "Almost well!" What a perspective! Mr. Baxter believed—and knew!—that death meant simply to depart and be with Jesus. According to God's Word, death is not the end, not the unknown, not the worst thing that can happen.

God's suffering servant Paul shows us how to live, but he also shows us how to die: "For to me, to live is Christ, and to die is gain" (Philippians 1:21). Paul yearned to be with the Lord he loved. Yet he knew that each day he lived was another day to serve Christ. What an example for you and me!

Won't you make Philippians 1:21 your creed for life and death? Life is more than planning for retirement, saving money, purchasing a recreational vehicle, traveling, and living it up. Life is about living for and in Christ every day you are able. It's about looking ahead with hope and longing to that day when you will be in the presence of the Lord forever.

> *Lord, I want each day to count for Your glory. Give me strength to be a good witness of You to others. I long to live abundantly in You on this earth and then be in heaven with You. I echo Paul's thought: "to live is Christ, and to die is gain." Amen.*

Respecting the Authority of Others

Submit yourselves for the Lord's sake to every authority
instituted among men: whether to the king, as the supreme
authority, or to governors, who are sent by him to punish
those who do wrong and to commend those who do right.

1 PETER 2:13-14 NIV

Oh dear. Heads up! The word *submit* is coming at you. Does
this tiny six-letter word raise your heart rate? It certainly raises a
ruckus in our society. Before you think I'm singling you out for
this topic, know that this concept of submission to authority has
been with us from the opening pages of the Bible. Submission
is such a vital concept from God. We are to submit ourselves to
those in authority, which includes the government.

Specifically, what does the command to submit mean? Think
through this list of definitions. *Submit* means...

- ☞ "to rank oneself under"
- ☞ "to accept the authority" of another
- ☞ to "respect" the rank and God-ordained authority of
  another
- ☞ "to arrange in military fashion under a commander"
- ☞ "to put oneself in an attitude of submission"

Can you think of ways and areas in daily life where you can, do, and must submit to your country, state, local leadership, and personal relationships?

As Christians, called and set apart by God, we're passing through this world on our way to heaven. And yet we must maintain honorable social conduct as we live among others. I've found that I have an easier time doing something that doesn't come naturally when I know *why* it needs to be done. And this is true with submission. God tells you and me to "submit," but He also clearly tells us why. Did you notice these words in today's passage: "for the Lord's sake"? Could any answer to the question "Why?" be bigger or matter more?

The *why* of our submission is wrapped up in the *who* of our submission—God. You see, *God* is asking us to submit for His sake. He explains that submission is His will. So He's asking us to serve Him in our submission to others.

And here's another thought: *God is sovereign.* He knows all about the existing governments and officials. He's ordained and put them in authority (Romans 13:1-7). He also knows what He is accomplishing in His grand plan through these officials. Discover the comfort and power of simply trusting the Lord. As servants of God, and knowing it is His will and for His sake, submit.

> *Lord, understanding what submission is helps me see more clearly how important it is to honor You and respect the authority of others by being a person of submission. Help me have a willing spirit and a servant's heart as I accept Your authority and put submission into practice in my daily life. Amen.*

Following Those Who Follow the Lord

Join with others in following my example, brothers, and take note of those who live according to the pattern we gave you. For, as I have often told you before and now say again even with tears, many live as enemies of the cross of Christ. Their destiny is destruction, their god is their stomach, and their glory is in their shame. Their mind is on earthly things.

PHILIPPIANS 3:17-19 NIV

Don't you wish people wore big signs that flashed descriptions of their character? It would save us a lot of heartbreak if we could know ahead of time that someone is deceptive, selfish, or ungodly. Since this isn't a possibility, the next best thing is to develop discernment so we can get clues to a person's character and heart so we can associate with those who follow the Lord.

God's wonderful servant Paul shares wisdom on who we are to emulate. He sketches two pictures: friends of the cross and enemies of the cross.

Those who are *against the cross of Christ* can be known by their motives. They are self-focused, desiring to get their needs satisfied. They seek glory. They focus on the world's offerings.

Friends of the cross of Christ are known by their actions and hearts as they faithfully and earnestly follow Jesus Christ. Do you currently know and look to Christians who are pursuing the pattern set by Jesus and Paul? Are you that person for others to learn from?

From God's Word to Your Heart

There are so many messages for you and me in our three verses, Philippians 3:17-19.

Follow Christians. You're blessed if there is someone in your life who shows you how to follow in Christ's footsteps. If you're new to the faith, beseech God to lead you...quickly!...to someone who is looking to the Lord and following hard after Him (Psalm 63:8).

Model Jesus. I pray you'll take on the challenge of being one who models for others what it means to be a true follower of Jesus. I pray that you'll be able to say along with Paul, "Imitate me, just as I also imitate Christ" (1 Corinthians 11:1).

Stay alert. We've been warned to look for and recognize those who are enemies of Jesus. Paul wept when he spoke of those who choose to walk away from the Lord. Be sure you follow those who follow the Lord.

Be encouraged. As believers, we will see Jesus! We will be transformed into His image.

Paul's guidelines to discernment help us examine the hearts and lives of others...and ourselves. How is the cross of Christ making a difference in your daily life?

> *God, as I keep my eyes on You and my heart focused on Your Word, I will look to those who follow You for guidance. I'm "a friend of the cross," and I want to lead others to You. Help me do that. Amen.*

The Good Fight

But you, O man of God, flee these things and pursue
righteousness, godliness, faith, love, patience, gentleness.
Fight the good fight of faith, lay hold on eternal life, to
which you were also called and have confessed the good
confession in the presence of many witnesses.

1 Timothy 6:11-12

Have you worked out? Are you feeling strong? Are you ready
to fight the "good fight of faith"? I hope so! Paul urges us to *fight,*
to *struggle,* to *flee,* and to *pursue.* It sounds like we're training
to be in a new action series, but Paul's goal is much more godly.
We are to fight for something most worthy—the Christian faith.
With Paul as our coach, I think we'll be prepared.

Command 1: Flee the things of the world. Prior to these verses,
Paul specifically addressed the dangers of the love of money. When
we turn and flee from evil, we can run toward God and embrace
His priorities and purposes.

Command 2: Pursue godly things. Focus on righteousness, godliness, faith, love, patience, and gentleness.

Command 3: Fight the good fight of faith. Make your confession of faith before others. Letting the world know Whose you
are and Who you serve will make it easier for you to stay strong.
There's accountability when you stand for something!

Do words such as *flee* and *pursue* describe your flight *away* from the love of money and *toward* the godly attitudes of the Christian life? What steps can you take that would intensify the seriousness of these two actions in your daily life? "Fighting the good fight of faith" is a long-term battle. Coach Paul says we should fight until our Lord Jesus Christ's appearing. Perhaps if we are *fleeing* and *following* and *fighting* hard enough, we'll yearn more passionately for His return.

From God's Word to Your Heart

Paul's heart is certainly riveted on the Lord. As he longs for his Lord's second coming, Paul breaks forth in a roll call of God's attributes:

> Keep this commandment...until our Lord Jesus Christ's appearing, which He will manifest in His own time, He who is the blessed and only Potentate, the King of kings and Lord of lords, who alone has immortality, dwelling in unapproachable light, whom no man has seen or can see, to whom be honor and everlasting power (1 Timothy 6:14-16).

Yes, Paul's vision is elsewhere—not on temporal "things" such as money and possessions. In the midst of fighting his own fight for the faith, his focus is on godliness, on eternal life, on the fact of God's presence, on Jesus Christ, on His second coming, on the King of kings and Lord of lords, on immortality, on the unapproachable light, on the everlasting!

Where are your sights set, my friend? As a woman after God's own heart, you are to seek those things that are above and set your mind on things above (Colossians 3:1-2). Let's look upward together!

> *God, I'm looking upward and keeping my eyes on my victory in You. Prepare me and instruct me for this faith fight so I can keep my eyes on You. Amen.*

Looking at Your Heart

You lust and do not have. You murder and covet
and cannot obtain. You fight and war. Yet you do
not have because you do not ask. You ask and do not
receive, because you ask amiss, that you
may spend it on your pleasures.

JAMES 4:2-3

War and *peace*. I know these words make up the title of a classic novel, but they also indicate two conditions in the church. They can also describe the conditions of our hearts. When James writes this pretty blunt list of problems, he reveals the futility of these actions and behaviors. When we engage in those activities, we don't achieve what we're really after, and we certainly don't honor God.

As we look more closely at our hearts, James' terms will help us grow in our understanding of sin and evil, problems and solutions.

- *Wars.* James' first word to us is based on a Greek word used in a literal sense for armed conflict and in a figurative sense for strife, conflict, or quarreling.

- *Fights.* This is more of the same—battles, quarrels, and disputes. These are outbursts of hostility and antagonism.

- *Desires for pleasure.* Ah, this is where James puts his finger on the causes of warring and fighting. He says the problem is inside—inside the heart where the selfish desire to fulfill every personal pleasure and passion festers.

- *Lust.* Lust is a strong, passionate, unhealthy desire or longing. And because lust can't bring inward peace, it results in unrest and discontent, which often spills onto others.

- *Murder.* The craving for pleasure and the inability to achieve it can drive people to shameful deeds—even hatred and murder.

- *Covet.* Unchecked and uncontrolled desires can lead to extreme violence.

From God's Word to Your Heart

Through selfless prayer, you can give all your areas of strife and conflict to God. When the inside of your heart is free of selfish desire, you will not crave combat and deception. Instead, you'll hunger for God's peace.

Do you know, there's a "right" way to pray and a "wrong" way? The wrong way is to not pray at all. Another wrong way is to ask for things related to lustful desires or selfish wants instead of what will further God's will and purposes for you. One more wrong way is to ask for the wrong reasons. For instance, do you want to impress someone or are you sincerely seeking to benefit God and His plan?

Lift your motives before the Lord. Acknowledge any sinful thoughts and adjust them to match God's good and perfect will.

This echoes what He tells us in His Word regarding what pleases Him. Prayer, dear reader, is the beginning of the solution to the problem of strife.

> *Lord, examine my heart. Reveal the strife and selfish desires that counter my quest for Your peace. Help me get rid of those attitudes and embrace Your perspective. Amen.*

Growing in Grace

Adulterers and adulteresses! Do you not know that
friendship with the world is enmity with God?
Whoever therefore wants to be a friend of the world makes
himself an enemy of God.

JAMES 4:4

So many times we think small things don't matter. There's no harm in them. We think there's no way something of such little consequence in this life could hurt us at all. Perhaps it's being friends with one person who's a little on the edge. Or maybe just one date with an unbeliever. Just one small expenditure. Yet one small thing can be the first tiny move toward what James labels "friendship with the world." If a bathroom sink springs a leak, you could say, "It's just one leak...nothing will come of it." But something will come of it—disaster! First the area around the leak will become saturated, and before you know it, tiles will pop out of place, wood will expand and warp, rot will set in, and the damage will expand through the floor.

In today's verse, did reading the words *adulterers* and *adulteresses* shock you? James is deliberately shaking up the thinking of his readers who are spiritually unfaithful to God and who are making pleasure their chief concern. They *are* adulterers because they're not being faithful to God. They flirt with worldliness and with the pleasures of this world.

Don't forsake God! Each day make the choice to engage with and draw closer to Him.

Before today had you ever thought about this either/or choice? That you're choosing to be *either* a friend to the world *or* a friend to God? That you're choosing to be *either* an enemy toward the world *or* an enemy toward God? Search your heart and consider the kinds of choices you've made during the past hour...week... year. According to the pattern of your choices, are you building friendship with God or with the world?

God yearns to see His Spirit evidenced in your life. When you are humbly seeking to live wholly for Him, you'll receive the gracious help you need so you can do just that. God blesses the humble-minded and favors the lowly with His continual grace for continual growth. Make a point to pray for ways you can humbly seek a life that pleases God and ask for the assistance of His great and marvelous grace.

When you turn your eyes to Jesus, you won't be interested in the small trinkets that the world offers. When you turn your eyes to Jesus, you'll be consumed with *Him*—the light of His glory and grace. So turn your eyes to Jesus today.

> *Lord, I fix my eyes on You. I seek Your heart. Help me see where and how I've been flirting with the world. I won't let "it's just one time" become my mindset. I want to turn my attention and my thoughts and my actions toward eternity with You. I can't wait! Amen.*

Striving Together

Let your conduct be worthy of the gospel of Christ,
so that whether I come and see you or am absent,
I may hear of your affairs, that you stand fast
in one spirit, with one mind striving together
for the faith of the gospel.

PHILIPPIANS 1:27

Have you heard about the process that makes Dresden china so exquisite and so desirable? It's the fire. This magnificent porcelain, the world's finest, is fired three times—a process that brings out the gold and the crimson more beautifully and permanently fuses them to the china.

In a similar way the Christian is refined by fire. There are some privileges that come to Christians who faithfully follow Jesus. Let's look at two of them: *belief* and *suffering*. It's hard to think of suffering as a benefit, isn't it? But when we suffer for Christ, it *is* a blessing. How can we handle persecution?

- *Stand fast.* This is the correct posture for suffering. We aren't to be sitting, slouching, leaning, or lying down. Oh no! We are to stand fast—solid in our faith.

- *Strive together.* Pain and suffering and persecution should come from outside the body of Christ—not from the inside. Our quarrels should not be among ourselves. Instead, Christians are to strive together, side-by-side, with boldness and unity.

- *Shun fear.* We are not to be afraid when we suffer persecution and mistreatment.

As you look to the Lord in your suffering, I encourage you to remain strong in Him, standing fast, striving together with other believers, and shunning fear.

From God's Word to Your Heart

Strong faith stands up well in persecution. It withstands the pressure of trials. Just as an athlete strengthens his or her muscles through the discipline of a regular regimen, so you and I can nurture a stronger faith that will enable us to conduct ourselves in a way that is worthy of Christ. What do we need to do?

- Read God's Word regularly.
- Pray for greater faith.
- Read biographies of Christians that will inspire our faith and perseverance.

We need to trust God during the times of refining fire. By standing firm during these struggles, our commitment to Christ will be deepened, our faith will be strengthened, our passion to live for Him will be ignited, and our conduct will be worthy. Depend on God and trust Him to bring about His good and perfect will in your trial.

God, when I face those who oppose my faith and speak against Your way, give me the strength and boldness to stand fast. Help me see the struggle as a privilege because it draws me closer to You and the purpose You have for me. Amen.

Praying Constantly

Elijah was a man with a nature like ours, and he prayed earnestly
that it would not rain; and it did not rain on the land for three
years and six months. And he prayed again, and the heaven gave
rain, and the earth produced its fruit.

JAMES 5:17-18

I know that as a woman who seeks the truths of God's Word
for her life, you desire to make prayer a vital part of your daily
life. So do I. Let's sit at James' feet for an important message on
the power of righteous praying. Oh, what we can learn in these
few verses as James calls everyone in the church to prayer! That
includes those who are...

...*suffering.* When people are persecuted or facing trials, they
are to voice their prayers...their cries for help.

...*cheerful.* Those with cheerful attitudes are to sing praises—
another form of prayer.

...*sick.* When there is illness, the one who is sick is to call for
the leaders or elders of the church. The leaders are to pray
for the sick person.

...*sinful.* Believers are to confess their sins to God and pray for
each other. We are to be accountable to other Christians.

...*prayerful.* We're also called to care, to listen, and to pray
for others.

James is just like a doctor who always knows what's best—even though it hurts. When we have a physical ailment, sometimes the treatment is painful. Surgery sets us back. Chemotherapy and radiation knock us down. Even stitches and injections hurt. Yet in the end we're helped and relieved. Progress is made. That's what James (and the Lord) wants for you and me—to help us be rid of sin because it harms us. And sometimes the treatment hurts. It's difficult to admit mistakes, to ask for prayer, and to seek forgiveness. But in the end we are better people...and often we avoid more severe chastisement.

God is calling us to walk uprightly, admit our sin when we fail and fall, appeal to others for their prayers on our behalf, and to do the same for others—praying always.

Where does your life find you today? Are you suffering...or are you cheerful? Are you ill...or are you praying for someone who is? Pray constantly! Let God hear your prayers. At every turn. In every situation. For every need.

> *Lord, my heart longs to be in Your presence. When I face adversity, temptation, illness, worries, and times of gladness...I will lift up my words and my life to You. Amen.*

Living Up to Your Calling

I, therefore, the prisoner of the Lord, beseech you to
walk worthy of the calling with which you were called,
with all lowliness and gentleness, with longsuffering,
bearing with one another in love, endeavoring to keep
the unity of the Spirit in the bond of peace.

EPHESIANS 4:1-3

As a child I remember my parents saying to my three brothers
and me, "With privilege comes responsibility." Later, as a parent,
I heard myself passing this wisdom on to my two daughters.

You, dear friend, have been abundantly blessed by God. And
such blessing and privilege should evoke an overwhelming sense
of responsibility. The duties and behaviors that will define your
life in light of such blessings will lead you to "the worthy walk"
to which you are called. This walk will lead you from studying
principles to putting them into practice, from reflecting on your
position in Christ to committing to your pursuits as a follower
of Christ, from knowledge of doctrine to a sense of duty.

As you discover and embrace God's calling and live out the
grace He has so marvelously bestowed on you, you're helping
to unite the body of Christ. Nurture godly attitudes in Christ,
including:

- *lowliness*—the practice of looking at others as more important than yourself
- *gentleness*—the practice of meekness and being mild-spirited and self-controlled
- *longsuffering*—the practice of resolved patience and the ability to endure discomfort without fighting back
- *forbearance*—extending a heart of love, handling the faults and failures of others, and refusing to avenge wrongs

These godly attitudes might at first sound like being weak, especially in the world we live in. But when they come from a heart given to God, they become demonstrations of great faith. Have you been patient with someone who is very difficult? Have you pressed on without blaming or condemning someone who made a mistake that cost you time or opportunity? Have you put another's interests ahead of your own without drawing attention or complaining? Each of these responses takes the strength and grace of God.

From God's Word to Your Heart

You bear a great label—"Christian"—and have a great responsibility to live up to it. There's a story about a soldier in Alexander the Great's army. The man was called up to be court-martialed for desertion. "What's your name?" asked Alexander the Great. "Alexander," was the man's reply. "Then change your name or change your ways," the king commanded.

Our conduct is an advertisement for or against Jesus Christ. That's why unity in the body of Christ is so important. Jesus prayed that His disciples (and the church) would live out their calling and be unified. By the sustaining power of God's Spirit, you can work toward unity in the faith.

Lord, I want to be a billboard for You in everything I do. Help me respond to others with grace and kindness and compassion. I want to be worthy of my calling in You. Amen.

Counting the Cost

Then [Jesus] said to them all, "If anyone desires
to come after Me, let him deny himself, and
take up his cross daily, and follow Me."

LUKE 9:23

Don't you hate dealing with high-pressure salespeople? If you're like me, you get flustered. I usually can't think. I feel intimidated. I often end up making a bad decision or buying something I don't want or don't like.

Well, Jesus was definitely not a high-pressure salesman. In fact, His methods ran in the opposite direction. He asked people to count the cost of following Him. Aside from the command "Follow Me," Jesus said, "Whoever loses his life for My sake will save it" (Luke 9:24). No gimmicks, no deceptions, and no discounts...just the life-transforming truth.

People in marketing today might ask, "How can we make following Jesus simpler? How can we make it sound like the cost isn't that high?" But Jesus wasn't looking for those who would follow Him because it was easy or convenient. He was looking for those who would count the cost and then choose to follow Him, no matter what sacrifices were needed up front and along the way:

And whoever does not bear his cross and come after Me

cannot be My disciple. For which of you, intending to build a tower, does not sit down first and count the cost, whether he has enough to finish it…So likewise, whoever of you does not forsake all that he has cannot be My disciple (Luke 14:27-28).

The roll call of Jesus' followers is convicting and thought provoking. John the Baptist, for instance, was beheaded. A boy in one of the crowds gave up his sack lunch of bread and fish (and Jesus used it to feed more than 5000!). Many of the disciples carried on Jesus' message and suffered disgrace and death for Him.

And Jesus calls you and me to do likewise. We need to sacrifice our pride, possessions, arrogance, and selfishness. And we should give up our excuses too. Following Jesus requires sacrifice, and He doesn't want anyone to be surprised about that so He tells us to count the cost.

From God's Word to Your Heart

I'm sure you've discovered that success comes with a price. It's no different in the Christian life. Jesus freely let people leave who weren't willing to pay the price of following Him. He cautioned one person who wanted to delay following Him, "No one, having put his hand to the plow, and looking back, is fit for the kingdom of God" (Luke 9:62).

Being a disciple of Christ isn't a one-time transaction. Jesus was asking His followers—and is asking you and me—to count the cost on a daily basis as we live for Him. Invest in those things that will last. It isn't easy to pick up your cross and follow Jesus, but when you do, your purpose unfolds and your life is filled with joy and significance.

Lord, I want to follow You no matter what it costs. With Your strength and grace, I will let go of any qualities, possessions, and attitudes that stand between me and Your way. Help me willingly pick up my cross and dedicate my life to You. Amen.

Praying God's Way

I exhort first of all that supplications, prayers, intercessions,
and giving of thanks be made for all men, for kings and
all who are in authority…[For God] desires all men to be
saved and to come to the knowledge of the truth.

1 TIMOTHY 2:2,4

Have you genuinely prayed for someone who was against
you? Imagine living in a country where the leaders are not Christians—and, in fact, are hostile to the Christian faith. Would
you pray for them? That's what was beginning to take place all
over the Roman Empire at the time this letter was written to
Timothy. Leaders across the empire were beginning to take note
of Christianity as being non-Jewish and anti-emperor worship.
As a result, the leaders were starting campaigns of persecution
against the followers of Jesus Christ.

Then imagine your pastor asks you to pray for these people—the
very ones who are oppressing you and your brothers and sisters
in Christ—regardless of how murderous or evil they are. How
would you respond? *Could* you do it? *Would* you do it? I hope you
said yes because that's what today's verses tell us to do. Timothy
reveals the kinds of prayers we and the church are to be engaged in:

- ☞ *supplications*—from a Greek word meaning "to lack,"
  this kind of prayer occurs because of a need. We request
  from God.

- *intercessions*—we approach God in confident, familiar prayer. The word *intercession* suggests personal and confiding conversation with God on behalf of others.
- *Giving thanks*—thanksgiving is the complement of true prayer. All our supplications, prayers, and intercessions are to be offered with a spirit of gratitude.

Are any of these aspects lacking in your prayer life today? If so, incorporate them into your time with God, and become a woman devoted to prayer.

From God's Word to Your Heart

Praying God's way for the leaders of our country—whether they're hostile to or supportive of Christianity—can make a difference in their lives, in our country, in our churches, and in our lives. Prayer change *things,* but prayer also changes *us.*

So pray. Pray for governmental officials. Pray for those in authority. Pray for your church leadership. Pray for your friends. Pray for your enemies (Luke 6:28). And, dear woman (and wife and mother and daughter and sister and aunt), follow after God's own heart and *pray* fervently for your family. *Give thanks* for those in your family circle who love the Lord Jesus Christ. *Intercede* for your loved ones. *Commit* to impassioned *supplication* for your spouse...or child...or mother or father...or brother or sister... who doesn't embrace Jesus.

> *God, it is a great privilege and blessing to be able to come to You about the people I love...and even those who persecute me. Fill my heart with love and compassion and hope as I lift up prayers of supplication, intercession, and thanksgiving. Amen.*

Giving to Others

> Do not let a widow under sixty years old be taken into the
> number, and not unless she has been the wife of one man,
> well reported for good works: if she has brought up children,
> if she has lodged strangers, if she has washed the saints' feet,
> if she has relieved the afflicted, if she has diligently followed
> every good work.
>
> 1 TIMOTHY 5:9-10

How can a woman know beyond a shadow of a doubt that her life has counted? Today's lesson gives us a checklist for godly character and a life of good works. Let's hurry on and find out what the Lord's standards are for those who, like you and me, yearn to lead a lovely and useful life.

Although Paul presents the qualities of an honorable widow, we can view his description as a model for every woman, no matter her season or station in life. Explore the attributes of this woman. How do you match up?

- *Faithful to her husband*—Do you honor and respect your husband?

- *Known for her good works, including parenting*—If you're a mom, do you view that privileged role as a good work? It is!

- *Practices hospitality*—Do you welcome friends and strangers into your home?

- *Humbly serves the saints*—Do you show humility through service at home, work, church, and in your community?

- *Helps the afflicted*—Do you lend a helping hand? Who can use your help? How about a single mom who could use an afternoon of childcare? Is there someone sick or lonely who could use a visit?

- *Pursues every good work*—Do you seek out ways to serve and follow through with good deeds?

Pursuing godliness means pursuing all of these attributes. Is such a godly goal on the top of your daily "to do" list?

From God's Word to Your Heart

I could go on and on in praise of these verses and what they've meant to me as a woman. It's what I call one of the "pink passages" of the Bible—one of the sections in God's Word that spells out for women after God's own heart exactly what it means to be a true woman of excellence. Verse 10 especially shows us God's priorities, God's standard and design for our everyday lives: "If she has brought up children, if she has lodged strangers, if she has washed the saints' feet, if she has relieved the afflicted, if she has diligently followed every good work." God calls us to a life of service.

Take a look at what you're currently doing. In what areas do you shine? In what areas could you use some improvement? Pray about both areas, dedicating yourself to God and to service in His name. There is goodness and godliness in a life of service to others.

Lord, I want my life to count. May my mission and vision be to serve You and others and to pursue good works with passion and sincerity. Amen.

Achieving Victory

Humble yourselves under the mighty hand of God,
that He may exalt you in due time, casting all your care
upon Him, for He cares for you.

1 PETER 5:6-7

Do you live a victorious life? You can through Christ! Victory is yours when you understand your Master, your enemy, and your fellow believers.

What kind of Master do you have? God is mighty and caring. He's trustworthy. You can count on Him in everything. There is never a reason to cower or despair. God is with you!

What kind of enemy do you have? The devil is dangerous. He is continually on the prowl. Beware of him! Never let your guard down.

What about your fellow sojourners in Christ? Some are suffering. Pray for them. And remember they are praying for you.

What comfort and encouragement you and I can draw from this information! As we face our foes and endure mistreatment and misunderstanding, we can *look* to God, *look out* for the devil, and *look outside* ourselves in concern for our brothers and sisters.

As you think about your life, how does the promise that God will exalt you ease your difficulties? Are you comforted because you know God cares for you? Do you cling to that truth when troubles come?

You will never be alone in your suffering. God is your constant companion. And you won't ever be the only one who suffers. Peter said every brother and sister in Christ around the globe experiences the same sufferings you and I do (1 Peter 5:9). Have you thought about expanding your prayer life to include other suffering saints?

From God's Word to Your Heart

I've shared with you before about my husband's involvement in the Army Reserves. No army ever gets a job done without the cooperation, obedience, and quick responses of its soldiers. And with wisdom from Peter, we also understand that no army ever wins a battle without understanding the enemy.

Whether we like it or not, Christians have always been compared to soldiers, and the battle that we wage against sin and evil has been likened to war. To adequately wage the war God calls us to fight, we need God's help. We need motivation, training, discipline, and endurance. Achieving victory also demands that we be unified and aggressive. Unity is accomplished as we submit to one another, and aggression is expressed as we resist the devil and the forces of evil.

God, I'm so humbled and amazed that You care about me so deeply. What a relief that I can cast my cares upon You and know that You are with me through each trial. Help me stay alert and watch for the enemy. Guide me as I take steps to unite with my brothers and sisters in Christ. Give me a warrior's heart and strength. Amen.

Bloom Where You're Planted

I want you to know, brethren, that the things
which happened to me have actually turned out
for the furtherance of the gospel, so that it has become
evident to the whole palace guard, and
to all the rest, that my chains are in Christ.

PHILIPPIANS 1:12-13

Do you complain about your circumstances at times? Do you wish you lived in a different state or neighborhood or had a different job? Have you lamented decisions you made or mourned trials that resulted in where you stand today? We've all done these things at one time or another. But we can follow Paul's example and choose to bloom where we're planted. He did—even when he was in prison.

Paul saw the blessings of his situation. From prison he could serve God as a witness to the Roman guards who watched over him day in and day out. He wrote letters and communicated through friends so he could be an inspiration and teacher for the churches. He was an example of boldness and faithfulness to those who feared persecution because of their faith in Christ.

My friend, are you chained to something? Or, to put it another way, what are your divinely appointed circumstances? Are you a wife, a mom, a single woman, a widow, a homemaker, an employee? Consider how your situation is a blessing, and how your circumstances can help you serve Christ and further His cause.

Where does today find you? I want to leave you with yet a few more words—powerful words—from Paul. He wrote these uplifting lines in Romans 8:28-29: "And we know that all things work together for good to those who love God, to those who are the called according to His purpose. For whom He foreknew, He also predestined to be conformed to the image of His Son." Knowing God and trusting in His promise to work all things together for good makes us women of hope. Our God is in control of all things—even those things that appear to be negative.

When we choose to bloom where our all-wise God plants us, we will one day be able to declare with Paul, "I want you to know, brethren, that the things which happened to me have actually turned out for the furtherance of the gospel."

> *God, help me accept where I am now and see the blessings and opportunities that are right here. I trust in You for my life. May I embrace what You're doing in my life so I can share with others the wonders of Your great purposes. Amen.*

Responding to the Savior

Then the angel said to them, "Do not be afraid, for behold,
I bring you good tidings of great joy which will be to all
people. For there is born to you this day in the city of
David a Savior, who is Christ the Lord. And this will be
the sign to you: You will find a Babe wrapped in swaddling
cloths, lying in a manger."

LUKE 2:10-12

Have you heard a group of elementary schoolchildren reciting "the Christmas story" from Luke? There's nothing like it! Many adults can recite the story right along with them. That's how familiar people are with the story of Jesus Christ's birth.

As we read the Bible, we quickly discover that God is a "seeking" God. He sought out individuals, including Adam, Noah, Abraham, Mary, and countless others to accomplish His plans and bless His people. We are inspired in our faith when we explore how others respond to Jesus. As we look to the shepherds in the field, they are at first afraid, but then their fear was transformed. What did they experience?

- *Belief.* The shepherds said, "Let us now go to Bethlehem and see this thing that has come to pass" (Luke 2:15). They didn't say, "Let's go see *if* this came to pass." They had believing hearts.

- *Motivation.* After hearing the news, the shepherds wanted to go immediately to Bethlehem. And once there, they shared their story with all who would listen (verse 17). Belief generated action.
- *Praise.* As the shepherds returned, they praised and glorified God for all that they had seen and heard (verse 20).

With faithful hearts, these shepherds responded to the good news of a Savior born in Bethlehem, acted on it, shared it with others, and praised God.

From God's Word to Your Heart

I believe a Christian woman's heart for God should be like a teakettle on a flaming stove burner—hot to the touch, visibly steaming, and audible. The heat of her love moves her to activity. Her passion for Christ—the object of her affection and enthusiasm—finds a voice. Everyone within earshot hears about the great things He who is mighty has done for her (Luke 1:49).

What's your response to the Savior? How audible is your passion for Jesus? And how intense is the heat of your love for Him? The presence of the Savior should inspire a fervent reaction in your soul. Does your passion for the Son of Man show? Are you glorifying and praising God for all you know and have heard? Are others hearing of your passion for Christ?

> *God, You seek my heart. May the truth of Christ turn my belief into action and praise. And may I always share with anyone who will hear the good news of You. Amen.*

Learning About God's Plan

Women adorn themselves in modest apparel, with propriety and moderation, not with braided hair or gold or pearls or costly clothing, but, which is proper for women professing godliness, with good works. Let a woman learn in silence with all submission. And I do not permit a woman to teach or to have authority over a man, but to be in silence.
For Adam was formed first, then Eve.

1 TIMOTHY 2:9-13

As we look through the window of God's Word we get to the heart of what it means to be a woman who pursues godliness. The world tries to pull our attention in many directions, but aren't you glad God gives us His plan in His Word? Paul, in his letter to Timothy, cuts right to the heart of things. By understanding the purposes and plans God has for His women, we can rest and flourish in our roles.

Regarding our appearance—Are you careful about what you wear? Have you explained God's dress code to your daughter or to the young women you mentor? Paul's portrait of godliness show us we're to be modest, moderate, proper, and godly.

Regarding our conduct—Women are to adorn themselves with that which is proper for women professing godliness: "with good works" (1 Timothy 2:9-10).

Regarding our roles—Paul's teaching concerning the role of women in the church is not based on the culture of his day or on Jewish culture. Instead, Paul points to the order of creation from Genesis (2:21-23). My friend, Paul's command has nothing to do with a woman's *spiritual* position. Men and women are equal before the Lord. It is for *earthly* relationships that Paul presents this order.

Are you thanking God for the opportunities to submit to His design for godliness and fulfill the different roles He is asking you to perform?

From God's Word to Your Heart

Thankfully, the book of Timothy places much emphasis on pursuing godliness, on actively striving for a reverential heart attitude that will be shown in our actions. And I'm sure you agree that as women of God, we can't claim to reverence and worship God and, at the same time, disregard His plan for our behavior and our roles.

From my heart to yours, here's what I (and Paul and God's Word) want for you and me, dear sister. Rather than struggling and wrangling over the issues of teaching or silence or submission in the church, we need to set our hearts and minds and efforts to work on showing by our ministry of good works—in the church and with our families at home—the reality of God's salvation in our lives. God *will* bless us as we pursue godliness in this way.

> *God, I will honor You with the way I dress, behave, and serve the church and my family. When the world confuses me about my roles or I become distracted, help me return to the focus and guidance of Your Word. Amen.*

To Bless or to Curse?

With it we bless our Lord and Father, and with it we curse
men, who have been made in the likeness of God.

JAMES 3:9 NASB

Take one guess as to what James is talking about in today's
verse. If you feel a twinge of conviction, you're probably zoned
in on the right answer: our tongues. It isn't easy to stay faithful
with the use of our words. We tend to speak carelessly about those
who are made in God's image. It's easy to express strong anger
or pride. But it isn't easy to stop such behavior. James said, "No
one can tame the tongue" (James 3:8 NASB). Before you get too
discouraged and give up, I hope it comforts you to know that
there is hope in the Holy Spirit!

When it comes to the tongue, James is appalled. He's flab-
bergasted. Why? Because he sees it used in such opposing ways.
Here is James' heart on the matter of the incredible tongue:

> Out of the same mouth proceed blessing and cursing. My
> brethren, these things ought not to be so. Does a spring
> send forth fresh water and bitter from the same opening?
> Can a fig tree, my brethren, bear olives, or a grapevine
> bear figs? Thus no spring can yield both salt water and
> fresh (James 3:10-12).

This is an eye-opening perspective. Why do we let something bad come from the same source that flows with something good? Let's make sure our choice of words, expressed thoughts, and the emotions behind our opinions come from a place of godliness and obedience…and then let that be all that flows from our mouths.

From God's Word to Your Heart

To bless or to curse? That's the question James raises about our speech. Only you can decide how to answer that in your life. Did you know that the word *gossip* is used in the Bible for the devil? His name is *diabolos,* which means "slanderer." In fact, in the Greek Scriptures, *diabolos* is used 34 times as a title for Satan and once to refer to Judas, who betrayed Jesus (John 6:70).

This is frightening company to be in. No woman who loves God wants to be part of that group. So purpose to not be a gossip or a slanderer (literally a "she-devil"). Jesus taught that the devil is a liar and the father of lies (John 8:44). And I'm sure you don't want to act like the devil, the accuser of the brethren and our adversary who "walks about like a roaring lion, seeking whom he may devour" (1 Peter 5:8).

To bless or to curse. It's your choice. Won't you choose to honor God and bless the people around you with sweet fruit from your lips?

Lord, forgive me for using my mouth to tear down others. I can't tame my tongue, but I can bring my heart, my speech, my tongue, and my need to gossip under the control of the Holy Spirit. I pray to be a speaker of life and light. I want to be a blessing to others and to Your name. Amen.

Thinking on God's Truths

Whatever things are true, whatever things are noble,
whatever things are just, whatever things are pure, whatever
things are lovely, whatever things are of good report, if
there is any virtue and if there is anything praiseworthy—
meditate on these things.

PHILIPPIANS 4:8

Do you know your thought life directly impacts your spiritual life? Are you familiar with the admonition, "Sow a thought, reap an action; sow an action, reap a habit; sow a habit, reap a character; sow a character, reap a destiny"? And how did destiny come to be? Well, it began with a thought.

And our thoughts are vital to finding peace. In his letter to believers in Philippi, Paul is pushing his readers (and us) to achieve inner peace so they will enjoy peace among themselves in the church. He knew that if inner tranquility is to be continually enjoyed and its influence spread, certain ingredients need to be present and make up the contents of our thoughts. We're to focus on what is...

- true (includes the gospel truth)
- noble (dignified, honorable, and worthy of honor)
- just (what is fair, morally upright, good)

- pure (morally undefiled)
- lovely (pleasing, attractive, winsome, good-will)
- of good report (speaking well of, something fit for God to hear)
- virtuous (excellent)
- praiseworthy (anything that garners God's approval, anything worthy of praise)

From God's Word to Your Heart

Adhering to the eight aspects of a Christian's thought life can seem overwhelming, especially if you try to do them all at once. To make these areas of importance part of your daily living, I came up with three "meditate on these things" you and I can focus on, knowing they meet the Philippians 4:8 criteria.

Meditate on God. When we contemplate the person of God and His attributes, we're pondering the riches of His wisdom, knowledge, goodness, and grace to us. Get excited about the many promises God extends to us...and follows through on.

Think about Jesus Christ. Oh, our sweet, sweet Savior! Recall the prophecies and plan of God that point to Jesus' coming to earth for our salvation. Reflect on the Gospel accounts of the life of Christ: His nativity, His death, His resurrection, His ascension. Lift your heart in praise for all He willingly did for you.

Think about the Word of God. As the psalmist declared, the law of the Lord is perfect, sure, right, pure, clean, true, righteous...and sweeter than honey and the honeycomb (Psalm 19:7-10). Focus on God's provision, care, love, great mercy, and grace.

When we spend our time thinking on these three lofty

"things"—God, His Son, and His Word—why would we want to think on anything else?

> *Lord, I worship You today. As I seek a peace-filled life, I will meditate on those things that are Your truth, that are good and holy. May the fruit of my thoughts and life be praiseworthy in Your eyes. Amen.*

Looking Forward to the End

In this you greatly rejoice, though now for a little while, if
need be, you have been grieved by various trials, that the
genuineness of your faith, being much more precious than
gold that perishes, though it is tested by fire, may be found
to praise, honor, and glory at the revelation of Jesus Christ.

1 PETER 1:6-7

How would you respond to an article or feature entitled "Three
Reasons Why You Can Stand Anything That Comes Your Way"?
To me it sounds like a bestseller! That's the kind of information
I want to grab. Well, dear friend, Peter has a powerful—and
hopeful!—message for us as we suffer for doing what's right.
He gives us three reasons why we can withstand anything that
comes our way.

Reason 1: We can stand anything because of what we are looking forward to—our magnificent inheritance of life with God.

Reason 2: We can stand anything if we remember that every
trial is a test…and trials make our faith stronger and more resilient.

Reason 3: We can stand anything because at the end of our
lives, when we're with Jesus Christ, we'll receive our rewards from
Him—His praise and glory and honor.

Christ extends marvelous grace and peace to us in every circumstance. Have you experienced this in your life? Revel in the

goodness of the Lord's provision. If your past has been free of such pain but you're grieved by current trials, remain joyous in the goodness of the Lord. It is in His strength and truth that you can stand strong and persevere.

From God's Word to Your Heart

I wish it weren't true, but suffering is a fact of life. It's just as Jesus declared: "In the world you will have tribulation" (John 16:33). But aren't you glad that Jesus went on to add, "But be of good cheer, I have overcome the world"? Peter was present when our Lord uttered these precious insights, and Peter's words to fellow believers reflect what he learned. Yes, there is suffering. But you can experience great joy in your trials when 1) your suffering is for doing what is right, and 2) when you look forward to spending time in Jesus' presence.

Friend, we've been given all things that pertain to life and to living life in a godly manner (2 Peter 1:3). And that "all things" includes the grace to endure suffering for doing what is right. So when trials come your way, look to the Lord! And look to the glory and joy He promises to give His suffering children.

Lord, You know the affliction I'm currently experiencing. My circumstances grieve me, but I'm holding on to the knowledge of Your provision. I will press on and do the right thing in Your name. I praise You each day. And when I've made it through this trial, I will give You even more praise and glory. Thank You for loving me. Amen.

Living Godly in an Ungodly World

He who is not with Me is against Me,
and he who does not gather with Me scatters.

Luke 11:23

If you're involved in any witnessing efforts, I'm sure you've seen a variety of reactions—positive and negative—to the truth about Jesus Christ. When people argue, put down, or condemn the gospel message, don't give up. Instead, be encouraged because Jesus experienced those reactions to His message—and to Him personally!—as He preached, worked miracles, and sought to redeem sinners. For instance, one group accused Him of having a demon, while another group sat on the fence to wait for more miraculous signs (John 7:20; 12:37).

There is an all-out battle being waged between good and evil, between God and Satan. And, my beloved, there is no middle ground when it comes to following Christ. We either strive to be godly or give in to ungodliness. So what can we do? Jesus tells us! We can pray...and we can take a firm stand for Christ. Jesus taught us how to pray, including the most important topics to lift up to Him:

- our relationship with God
- our worship
- our desire for God's will

- our dependence on God
- our confession of sin
- our weaknesses and need for God's help

Jesus said to pray...

> Our Father in heaven,
> Hallowed be Your name.
> Your kingdom come.
> Your will be done
> On earth as it is in heaven.
> Give us day by day our daily bread.
> And forgive us our sins,
> For we also forgive everyone who is
> indebted to us.
> And do not lead us into temptation,
> But deliver us from the evil one
> (Luke 11:2-4).

We are to pray for these things with conviction because, when it comes to Jesus, there is no neutrality! Christ's love for us is passionate and purposed.

From God's Word to Your Heart

Take the time to memorize, pray, and live the "Lord's prayer." In an ungodly world Jesus lived with fiery passion. His disciples were reminded daily of His zeal as they watched Him minister to people. Where did Jesus get His energy and enthusiasm? One answer is obvious—His habit of prayer.

Do you long for more passion in your Christian life? To be

more like Jesus? Then pray. As you make prayer a habit, you'll discover God's purpose for you. As you pray and choose to believe, your days will become pointed rather than pointless, full rather than empty, vibrant rather than lifeless.

Lord, through prayer I have Your power to stand strong when there is conflict, evil, resistance, and temptation. Thank You. Amen.

Living by the Holy Spirit

And do not be drunk with wine, in which is
dissipation; but be filled with the Spirit, speaking to
one another in psalms and hymns and spiritual songs,
singing and making melody in your heart to the Lord.

EPHESIANS 5:18-19

Recently I was visiting with my widowed sister-in-law. We were reminiscing through some of my brother's quips and sayings. He always had a slogan or motto for every occasion. One of them I applied just today as I wondered where to shop for a particular item. His saying guided me: "The place to go is the place you know."

In our Christian pursuits, we aren't looking for a place to shop. We're looking for ways to live Jesus. As children who walk in the light, we desire to be in the presence and under the influence of the Lord Jesus, letting His mind and His actions be ours. When we are under the influence of God's Spirit, we take on new, godly attitudes.

An attitude of joy and happiness—In the early church, Christians spoke words of encouragement through Old Testament psalms put to music. They also sang hymns and spiritual songs of praise and personal testimony. Let's follow their lead and reveal our joy as we participate in worship.

An attitude of thankfulness—Give thanks for salvation. We need to be faithful to recall and share our before-and-after stories to inspire others. Many believers joyfully give thanks to God for the good things that happen in their lives, but Paul says we are to "give thanks *always* for *all* things" (Ephesians 5:20). So let's hold on to a thankful spirit when it comes to setbacks, sufferings, and disappointments.

An attitude of submission—Jesus Christ was a humble, submissive servant to the Father. We want to follow in His footsteps in every relationship.

From God's Word to Your Heart

What Christian doesn't want to please God? As Jesus said, "If you love Me, keep My commandments" (John 14:15). How can you show your love for Christ? Paul gives you the answer in today's verses: "Be filled with the Spirit." When you choose to walk in obedience to God's Word, His Spirit will empower you to...

- give praise out of a joyful heart
- give thanks out of a grateful heart
- give honor to others out of a submissive heart

Aren't you continually in awe that the God of the universe indwells you and gives you guidance for every action when you submit your will to Him? I am! Go to the place you know—God's presence—and embrace the joy of your salvation.

> *Lord, I'm filled with awe because You are so faithful and all powerful. Joy springs up in my heart today because I know Your commands and love. I gladly follow You with all my heart. Amen.*

Caring for Others

Do not rebuke an older man, but exhort him as a father,
younger men as brothers, older women as mothers, younger
women as sisters, with all purity.

1 TIMOTHY 5:1-2

One Sunday, while looking at my church bulletin, I noticed the following announcement: "Biblical Counseling 101 will be offered. This is an in-depth discipleship class that will help you in your own walk with the Lord, so that you, in turn, can help others. If you're interested in attending, sign up with the pastor." My thought? Who wouldn't want to attend this class!

In 1 Timothy, Paul offers us similar instruction, and his lesson in today's verses is about two ways to approach those in the body of Christ who don't know they're doing something wrong or who are deliberately sinning.

- *Rebuke* literally means to strike or beat with a blow. Metaphorically it means to pound with words or to reprimand.

- *Exhort* means to come alongside someone to help them and strengthen them.

Which approach would you want someone to take when addressing a sin or conflict in your life? I think we all hope that someone would approach us with compassion and with the purpose to help. Bear this in mind when you follow Paul's wisdom and approach those in the body of Christ who need guidance.

As a woman pursuing godliness, keep your actions honorable and your intentions focused on building up the body of Christ.

And now for you and me, my friend. Our attitude toward people in the church is to be that of a caring, loving family member toward other family members...even when they sin and err. Yes, we are to hate their sins, but we are to love them.

And don't you agree that a loving heart attitude is at the core of caring for others? Jesus, the ultimate Counselor, said, "Out of the abundance of the heart the mouth speaks" (Matthew 12:34). It's true that we speak and act out of what is in our hearts. So how about a heart checkup? How's your heart when it comes to caring for others?

Do you...

> ...love one another (John 13:34-35)
>
> ...pray for one another (Ephesians 6:18)
>
> ...respect one another (Philippians 2:3-4)
>
> ...comfort one another (1 Thessalonians 5:11)
>
> ...edify one another (Romans 14:19)

How do you handle people? Do you have a tendency to strike harshly or scold with words? If you're a mom, how do you handle the "little people" in your home? I encourage you to build up your own walk with the Lord so that you can help others with gentle compassion. If you're interested, sign up with instructor Paul anytime you need a refresher course on caring.

Lord, help me have a loving heart attitude when I move alongside those who are sinning. Give me Your wisdom and encouraging words to share so I can help them. Amen.

Working Out Your Faith

But someone will say, "You have faith, and I have works."
Show me your faith without your works,
and I will show you my faith by my works.

JAMES 2:18

I once heard a pastor tell a story about making a deposit at one of his bank's regional branches. His wife told him exactly where the bank branch was located in the parking lot of a local mall. When he got there, he found that the bank wasn't theirs. It was a different bank. When he got home, they had quite a discussion, each insisting they were right. So they got into the car and drove to the mall to settle their dispute...only to find they were both right. The building in the parking lot housed two banks! The wife had never noticed the other bank's entrance on the opposite side of the structure, the side her husband had pulled up to, and the husband hadn't noticed their bank.

That's a nice way to settle a disagreement, isn't it? To discover that you're both right? That's what happens when we look at the role that "works" play in evidencing genuine faith (which is accomplished by Christ apart from any works). The apostle Paul emphasized justification by faith apart from works, while James emphasizes the fact that true saving faith will be accompanied by works. Many have seen this as a contradiction. But just like the man and wife who were each right about the bank, Paul and James are both right in their assessment of faith and works. They are not in disagreement. They are simply looking at faith and works from two different angles to prove two different points.

From God's Word to Your Heart

How do we become women of faith and exhibit faith in action? We can search for the answers by taking our questions straight to the source of knowledge and wisdom—God's Word.

Where does faith come from? The answer is *grace*—specifically God's grace. In Ephesians 2:8-10 we learn that by grace we are saved. And that grace is a gift from God. Faith is a work of God in our hearts.

How is faith nurtured and strengthened? Here are two surefire ways:

- *By reading the Word.* When we read the Bible, we see up close the trials, testing, and temptations people faced, how they faced each situation, what they did, and whether it was successful.
- *By hearing the Word.* God has given His church another kind of gift—gifted teachers—to help us grow in faith. Hearing the Bible taught and explained fuels our faith and motivation to learn more.

Make it a point to share the Word and back up its teachings with your works (actions). And when you talk about the gospel with someone, think of something you can also do for that person. That way you send a double message about faith in Jesus Christ.

> *Lord, I want my life to be a clear example of Your grace. Help me reach out to others and stand for righteousness. Guide me in Your wisdom so that I am a woman of faith—and action! Amen.*

Demonstrating a Heart of Love

If anyone among you wanders from the truth, and
someone turns him back, let him know that he who turns
a sinner from the error of his way will save a soul from
death and cover a multitude of sins.

JAMES 5:19-20

As much as we want to think all believers have a solid spiritual life and a good understanding of God's truths, that's just not reality. James knows, as God does, that there are those who wander from the truth among believers. There are people in every congregation who profess salvation but fail to live it. As James points out, there is partiality and judging, unbridled speech against others, strife and bickering. We see it in our churches and in Christian circles.

But James also has uplifting advice for us. He turns us from condemnation toward the better "works" of love. He calls us to pray for one another and to love enough and care enough to pursue (rather than judge and gossip about) those who are wandering. Demonstrating this kind of love helps the sinner turn from the error of his way and saves his soul from death. James says we're to go after those who are straying from the truth and show them the way back to Christ. And when we do, the blessings are threefold:

🕊 We assist a sinner to turn from the error of his way.

🕊 We assist God in saving a soul from death.

☞ We help to cover a multitude of sins.

So which will it be? Works of love…or works of loathing? Words of blessing…or words of cursing? Pursuit of the sinner… or passing judgment?

From God's Word to Your Heart

It's one thing to watch out for others, but a woman of faith must also watch out for herself. Have you heard the saying, "You're either moving forward or backward. There is no such thing as standing still in the Christian life"? What can hurt your spiritual growth more than anything? Doing nothing! Passivity can and does have a disastrous effect on spiritual growth.

Another way to wander from the truth is to actively turn away from what is best and choose what is second best. Are there any "second best" choices you're currently making or have made in the past that are leading you away from your love for Christ? How will you set your feet once again on the highway of the righteous? Your journey as a woman growing in faith should not be passive, and it cannot be in the direction opposite God's truths. Your journey needs to be of singular focus on God and taking actions that move you toward becoming a woman after God's own heart.

May the *works* of your faith match the *words* of your faith. May your walk align with your talk.

> Lord, please give me a heart that is sensitive to those who are straying from Your truth. Help me approach them with compassion and integrity. May my walk always align with my talk…and may both demonstrate a heart of love. Amen.

Giving Thanks for Others

I thank my God upon every remembrance of you,
always in every prayer of mine making request for you all
with joy...being confident of this very thing, that He who
has begun a good work in you will complete it
until the day of Jesus Christ.

PHILIPPIANS 1:3-4,6

Imagine sitting in chains...alone...separated from those you know and love...awaiting a verdict that will determine whether you live or die. This lonely and potentially fear-provoking condition describes Paul's situation when he wrote to the believers in Philippi. Yet Paul realized complete peace as he turned his thoughts heavenward and prayed for others.

This same remarkable peace can be yours too as you go through any difficulty. Many women sit alone—some for days and nights on end. Many of us spend large amounts of time apart from friends and loved ones. And countless women await verdicts (from cancer tests, from lawyers, from spouses, from employers) that might point their lives in new and sometimes perilous directions. Aren't you glad that God's Word shows us a marvelous way to experience God's perfect peace in the midst of our problems? Take note of three perspectives that brought great joy and peace of mind to Paul. And remember...they will do the same for you!

☞ *A positive attitude.* How do you normally think of others? Are you positive and gracious or picky and negative?

☞ *A promise to claim.* God has started and is completing a good work in you.

☞ *A passionate heart.* Paul says, "God is my witness, how greatly I long for you all with the affection of Jesus Christ" (Philippians 1:8). A passionate heart for God longs to be with others who also desire to serve God.

From God's Word to Your Heart

And Paul did another thing. He looked to God—our wonderful God who is the author and perfecter and finisher of all He begins, our omniscient God who sees the end product as perfect and complete. God saw the people in Paul's life as they would be, and Paul sought to do the same. We can rest in the same fact—that God sees those in our lives as they will be. And the same goes for us!

To experience the power of peace in every situation, begin with thanksgiving. Giving thanks is commanded by God. His Word tells us to give thanks *always* and for *all* things, in *everything* (1 Thessalonians 5:16-18). The giving of thanks is a decision on your part. And once you decide to do it, there will be a powerful effect on your attitude and your peace. "The peace of God, which surpasses all understanding" is indeed available to you (Philippians 4:7). With this gift in your life, you always have something to thank God for.

Lord, thank You for being the Author and Perfecter of my faith. Help me remember that my joy and peace are grounded in You...and not in my circumstances. Amen.

Changing Your Behavior

Let all bitterness, wrath, anger, clamor, and evil speaking be
put away from you, with all malice. And be kind
to one another, tenderhearted, forgiving one another,
even as God in Christ forgave you.

EPHESIANS 4:31-32

Years ago when Jim was a pharmaceutical salesman, his manager would occasionally join him as he made his rounds to the doctors' offices. Jim's boss had been a top salesman before becoming a manager. He was so knowledgeable that he often spoke in generalities, assuming Jim knew what he meant. I'm sure you can imagine some of the challenges this created for Jim. He wanted and needed the full picture, but he usually received only bits and pieces.

That's not the case with the apostle Paul. He is very specific as he lets us know we should act to change our behavior and live our new lives as followers of Jesus Christ.

Let's take a walk. We're strolling through a gallery lined with exquisite works of art. Instead of rushing through like many people do, we choose to linger…to study and appreciate each one. The works focus on how we are in Christ. Here is the lineup of the beautiful, positive behaviors God desires of us.

☞ *Honesty*—Speak truth with integrity.

- *Emotions*—Rid your heart of anger, and don't let anger fester.

- *Work*—Fulfill your obligations and put your energy toward activities that meet the needs of others. Don't waste time.

- *Speech*—Let your words impart grace and mercy to others.

- *Behavior*—Act and speak in ways that edify and delight the Holy Spirit.

- *Attitudes and actions*—Release bitterness and pettiness. Concentrate on building others up.

- *Relationships*—Be tenderhearted toward others and have a forgiving heart.

Through Christ in us, these attributes of beauty are what God sees when He looks at us and our lives. Say goodbye to the wrong attitudes and embrace the new you!

From God's Word to Your Heart

Some scriptures call for a heart response of prayer, thanksgiving, humility, and inspiration. Others call for action. I'm sure you know that when it comes to spiritual growth, you aren't on autopilot. You didn't instantly possess right attitudes or think right thoughts or make right decisions the instant you became a child of God. No, growth into Christlikeness is a process, a day-by-day progression. It requires listening to God's Spirit as He prompts, convicts, and encourages. Glorious results are sure to follow!

If you're obedient to follow Jesus' leading, you'll be continually changing from the inside—in your character, values, attitudes, perspectives, and motives. And, blessing upon blessings, these inner changes will be noticed by others, who will see Jesus Christ reflected in your transformed heart.

Lord, I'm listening for Your leading. I embrace the clear teachings of Your Word. Thank You for providing it and for letting it speak so directly to my heart. Help me step forward with integrity, compassion, selflessness, and generosity. Amen.

Counting Your Blessings

You are a chosen generation, a royal priesthood,
a holy nation, His own special people, that you may
proclaim the praises of Him who called you out of darkness
into His marvelous light.

1 PETER 2:9

Do you suffer from low self-esteem? Well, my dear sister in Christ, for a Christian this condition shouldn't apply. Why? Because of who we are and what we have in Jesus Christ. Indeed, the entire book of 1 Peter offers an impressive list of the benefits and privileges and assurances we enjoy as believers in Christ. Peter graciously points to one advantage after another...after another...that are ours as saints. Here are a few of our blessings in Christ from 1 Peter 1:2–2:5:

- We are sanctified.
- We have God's grace and peace.
- We are born again.
- We have an inheritance in heaven.
- We are kept by God unto salvation.
- We are redeemed by Jesus' blood.
- We are living stones in the house of God.

How's that for a list of blessings? And Peter has only just begun! God has done all this so that we can enjoy our redemption, share with others the excellencies and virtues and qualities of God, and lift our praises to Him. We are called to proclaim who God is and what He has done—by our conduct and by our words (Matthew 28:11). Are you doing everything you can to let people know who you are in Christ?

So what's all the fuss about self-image? I hope by now you know you've been blessed beyond measure. In the moments when you slump or fall into despair or discouragement, you need to remember who you are in Christ. You are never a nothing or a nobody. Who are you? Read today's verse, 1 Peter 2:9, again!

- You are a chosen generation.
- You are a royal priesthood.
- You are a holy nation.
- You are God's special people.

All of this was accomplished by Christ on your behalf. Although some people base their worth on accomplishments, as a Christian your identity is based on who you are in Christ. That is far more important and meaningful than money, success, education, and career. You've been chosen by God to be His very own. And as a child of God—as one who has been purchased with the precious blood of Christ—you have worth that can never be tallied. Thank God now! And make it a point to refuse to succumb to feelings and thoughts of inferiority.

> *Lord, forgive me for listening to my self-talk more than I pay attention to Your bold statements about my worth. I have value because I am Your child. Thank You! Amen.*

Serving in the Workplace

All who are under the yoke of slavery should consider their
masters worthy of full respect, so that God's name and our
teaching may not be slandered.

1 Timothy 6:1 niv

Timothy was blessed to have Paul around to give him insights
into dealing with tough issues. And aren't we blessed to have the
same instruction? We're also blessed that we live in a nation that
has abolished slavery. With that in mind, look at Paul's instruction for slaves with the intention of applying it to yourself as an
employee and as a servant of God.

In Paul's day, it's been estimated, half of the world's popula-
tion were slaves. The message of salvation appealed to slaves, and
many of them became believers. Some of the slaves used their
newfound freedom in Christ as an excuse to disobey their masters.
Paul explains God's way for slaves to serve in the workplace and
respond to their masters. And in our roles today, we can apply
his teachings. What do we need to do?

Honor others. Even as we embrace our freedom in Christ, we
are not to stop honoring our leaders, employers, and those in
authority.

Maintain a strong work ethic. We are called to a high standard.

"Whatever you do in word or deed, do all in the name of the Lord Jesus" (Colossians 3:17). The consequence for having a bad work ethic? "If anyone will not work, neither shall he eat" (2 Thessalonians 3:10).

Practice godly attitudes. Whether we are enslaved or free, employer or employee, we are called to righteous attitudes:

> Slaves, obey your earthly masters with respect and fear, and with sincerity of heart, just as you would obey Christ. Obey them not only to win their favor when their eye is on you, but like slaves of Christ, doing the will of God from your heart. Serve wholeheartedly, as if you were serving the Lord, not men, because you know that the Lord will reward everyone for whatever good he does, whether he is slave or free. And masters, treat your slaves in the same way. Do not threaten them, since you know that he who is both their Master and yours is in heaven, and there is no favoritism with him (Ephesians 6:5-9 NIV).

From God's Word to Your Heart

Work, whether in or out of the home, is important to God. Why? Because your attitude toward work is a reflection of your attitude toward Him. God asks you to do your work heartily unto Him. You're also to serve your employers wholeheartedly and treat your employees fairly and with respect. Your obedience or disobedience to God's directives in the area of the workplace is easily seen—and noted!—by others.

Are people getting an accurate picture of the reality of Jesus Christ through your life? If you're truly pursuing a life of godliness, they will see the gospel in you. You are a witness to Christ (Acts 1:8). So…what's the gospel according to your life?

Master, even when my task is a simple one, You call me to a high standard. May I always remember that I am serving You and being a witness for You. Amen.

Living in Obedience

If anyone is a hearer of the word and not a doer, he is like a man observing his natural face in a mirror; for he observes himself, goes away, and immediately forgets what kind of man he was. But he who...is not a forgetful hearer but a doer of the work, this one will be blessed in what he does.

JAMES 1:23-25

I can still remember one of the very first "baby steps" I took as a new Christian setting out on my quest for spiritual growth and a growing faith. Our church offered a series of evening classes, and I enrolled in the one listed as "Spiritual Boot Camp." I wanted to be shaped up, disciplined, and shown the basics. I needed to firm up my beliefs and make some serious changes.

James offers a sort of spiritual boot camp for all of us. His book is full of advice for growing, for changing behavior, for beefing up and shaping faith. And what I like best is that he tells it like it is. When he's done with us, we know exactly what to do and what not to do. Why not accept James' challenges to obediently live your life in Christ? To be a doer of the Word of God?

From God's Word to Your Heart

The Word of God produces regeneration, but it's also an active force in our sanctification, in our purification. But you must do more than acknowledge the Bible as truth. What else is required?

- *Receive the Word.* Be quick to hear and to listen when the Bible is being taught. Be slow to speak so that what you say edifies those who hear, accurately reflects the Scriptures, and honors the Lord.

- *Do and live the Word.* Put what you learn and know into practice daily.

- *Bridle your tongue.* Prayerfully plan a "fast"—a quiet time or a day of rest—for your tongue so you can hear and understand better. Put others first.

- *Visit people in distress.* Actively care about and for people who are less fortunate than you are. Ask what you can do to help and then follow through.

- *Live a godly lifestyle.* Keep yourself unstained and unspotted by the world. Strive to follow God's principles and live His love and grace.

Did you enjoy James' illustration of a man who looks in the mirror and does nothing about what he sees? Can you relate? God's Word is your mirror. Do you read it with a seeking heart as you see yourself for who you really are—blemishes, faults, and all? Oh, the beauty of a woman after God's own heart who lives in obedience—who puts her faith into action and controls her tongue, changes her behavior on the outside to honor God, and carries out God's guidelines on the inside!

> *Lord, I want to live my faith. Help me speak to and treat others in ways that reflect my living, active faith and commitment to You. Please encourage me as I press on through the changes I need to make so I become an even more faithful doer of Your Word. Amen.*

About the Author

Elizabeth George is a bestselling author whose passion is to teach the Bible in a way that changes women's lives. She has more than 7 million books in print, including *A Woman After God's Own Heart*® and *A Woman's Daily Walk with God.*

For information about Elizabeth, her books, and her ministry, and to sign up to receive her daily devotions, and to join her on Facebook and Twitter, visit her website at:

www.ElizabethGeorge.com

BIBLE STUDIES *for*

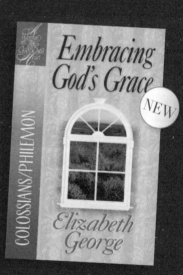